Amazing Facts You Don't Know

1100 Unbelievable Trivia Facts

---

volume 1

Compiled By

Michael Gonzalez

Table of Contents

Other Books
by Michael Gonzalez

Please check out these other fun trivia books
from the author:

Trivia Storm: 1,200 Exciting Trivia Questions
About Anything

Trivia Storm 2: 1,200 Exciting Questions
About Anything

Dedication

To my mother Miriam whose endless love and
support has made many things in my life
possible

Introduction

Amazing Facts You Don't Know is our go at presenting to you the joy of trivia in its simplest form: facts. It is the first of a series of trivia fact books dedicated to providing you with only the most jaw-dropping facts that you will have to look up on your own just to believe. Through a great deal of searching we have compiled 1,100 of only the most amazing facts commonly found in trivia. So take a break from trivia night, sit back and enjoy a book that will without a doubt surprise, amuse, and quite even shock you.

—Author Michael Gonzalez

Section One:
1–100

1-100

1.   *"Kalsarikännit"* is a Finnish word which means to get drunk in your underwear at home — with no intention of going out.

2.   A frustrated Stephen King threw the first pages of his novel *Carrie* into the trash but was urged by his wife to keep trying and continue on with it.

3.   A group of ferrets is called a *business*.

4.   A mall in China offers what they call "Husband Storage" — where wives can leave their husbands while they do their shopping.

5.   A strawberry is technically not a berry, but a banana is.

6.   A study done by neuroscientists at the University of California–Irvine found that people with a certain genetic variant are worse drivers than those with the 'normal' gene.

7.   About 100 people live in the Chernobyl exclusion zone.

8.   Albert Einstein never wore socks.

9.   An early proposed version of the Statue of Liberty was offered to Egypt as a gift by France but when it never came to be, a later design was given to America instead.

10.   Before being used by Nazi Germany, the swastika was a symbol of good luck and is still used today in Buddhism.

11.   Before he was famous, Kanye West worked at The Gap.

12.   Cats can get pregnant at four weeks old and can get pregnant again two weeks after giving birth.

13.   Charles Dickens gave every one of his 10 children nicknames like "Skittles" and "Plorn".

14.   Charlie Chaplin was the first actor to appear on the cover of *Time* magazine.

15.   Christopher Columbus was incarcerated upon his return to Spain for mistreating the natives of Hispaniola.

16.   Conan O'Brien and Andy Richter voiced two dock workers in the video game *Halo 4*.

17.   Congo was a chimpanzee that is considered the greatest animal painter in history. On June 20, 2005, 3 of his paintings were included in an auction alongside works by Renoir and Warhol and were sold for more than $26,000 USD.

18. Cyprus is one of only two countries to include the outline of the nation on their flag (with Kosovo being the other).

19. During "Respect for the Aged Day" in Japan, cigarette companies celebrate by giving senior citizens ten packs of cigarettes each.

20. Elephants are excellent swimmers.

21. Elvis Presley didn't create any of his own material, even the songs he was credited with writing.

22. Famous aviator Charles Lindbergh had 4 families. He had 3 separate, secret families and fathered a total of 7 children among them. Two of his wives were sisters, and the 3rd was his secretary. Some of his offspring only knew him by a fake name.

23. Flamingos are naturally white in color but turn pink because of the brine shrimp they eat — and the more shrimp in their diet, the pinker they become.

24. Former U.S. president Bill Clinton was asked to voice President John Eden in the video game *Fallout 3* but, sadly, declined.

25. Greenland is the least-densely populated country in the world.

26. Hares are born with fur while rabbits are born naked.

27. Having a late-night snack can cause nightmares, according to a study conducted by the University of Montreal.

28. Historically, the Japanese had the same word for blue as they did for green (青).

29. Hitler had intended to ban all slaughterhouses at the end of WWII

30. Hugh Hefner donated $900,000 USD to buy the land the Hollywood sign sits on before it could be bought by mansion developers.

31.   In 1894, as a four-year-old boy, Adolf Hitler was saved from drowning by a priest.

32.   In 1940, Hitler approved plans for the first sex doll after word reached him of a syphilis outbreak amongst German soldiers. However, the project was dropped after German soldiers refused to carry them around for fear of being caught with them by the enemy.

33.   In 1975, Napa, California used chickens to try and slow down traffic by allowing them to roam the streets.

34.   In 1985, a Soviet icebreaker ship, Moskva, rescued a pod of beluga whales trapped by pack ice by playing music and using it to lure them out through a cleared channel.

35.   In a study done by the Bradley Corporation, only 66% of Americans admitted to washing their hands after using a public washroom.

36.   In December 1914, Harry Houdini was summoned to a private meeting at the White House with President Woodrow Wilson, who told him, "I envy your ability of escaping out of tight places. Sometimes I wish I were able to do the same."

37.   In the 1950s, pregnant women were told it was safe to smoke during pregnancy.

38.   In the series *Fullmetal Alchemist*, all the men in Colonel Mustang's unit are named after mid-20th century aircraft.

39.   It is impossible to both swallow and breathe at the same time.

40.   James Cameron's *Avatar* was banned in China out of fear of it sparking an uprising.

41.   Kevlar®, Dyneema®, and Spectra Shield® can be pierced by an arrow — which can kill the wearer.

42. Korra from *The Legend of Korra* is the first bisexual heroine in an American children's series.

43. Lara Croft was originally going to be called Laura Cruz.

44. Leopards can stay in the same position for up to 8 hours.

45. Lt. "Mad" Jack Churchill was a British WWII soldier who was known to carry a longbow and a claymore sword.

46. Margaret Ann Bulkley dressed as a man for 56 years while she studied medicine and worked as a British Army doctor. Her secret was only discovered after her death.

47. Marilyn Monroe was on the cover of the first edition of *Playboy* magazine.

48. Metallica is the only band to have performed on all seven continents.

49.   Much of the Italian olive oil bought in stores are not in fact Italian.

50.   Nazi Germany had the strongest animal-rights laws to date and failure to comply with these laws would land you in a concentration camp.

51.   Nazi Germany were the first in modern history to launch an anti-smoking campaign.

52.   Nicolas Cage suggested Jonny Depp get involved in acting.

53.   On February 18, 1930, Elm Farm Ollie became the first cow to fly in an airplane.

54.   Only 2% of the earth's population has green eyes.

55.   Peregrine falcons are used by airports in the United States to help keep birds off the runway.

56.   Peter Benchley, who wrote the novel *Jaws*, was the speechwriter for U.S. president Lyndon B. Johnson.

57.   Pirate Rachel Wall was the last woman to be executed in the U.S. state of Massachusetts.

58.   Pirates were known to smuggle exotic birds such as parrots but, contrary to popular portrayal, never kept them as pets.

59.   Pokémon's creator, Satoshi Tajiri, is a high-functioning autistic.

60.   Queen Elizabeth II became the longest-reigning British monarch on 9 September 2015 when she surpassed the reign of her great-great-grandmother Victoria.

61.   Reportedly, Robert Luis Stevenson wrote *Dr. Jekyll and Mr. Hyde* while on a six-day cocaine binge.

62.   Ringneck parrots can age to 75 years.

63. Sean Connery was offered $10 million dollars and 15% box office takings to play Gandalf in *The Lord of the Rings* film.

64. Snails have teeth, and some are even capable of killing you.

65. Stephen King was so high on drugs and alcohol early in his career that he can't remember writing several novels, including *Cujo*.

66. Stephen King's iconic thriller *Carrie* was initially rejected by 30 different publishers before finally accepted.

67. The "fruit salad" tree is a tree that, through the process of horticultural grafting, grows more than one kind of fruit.

68. The *Back to the Future* film was rejected by Disney.

69. The chemicals found when passing gas are about 20%–90% nitrogen, 0%–50% hydrogen, 10%–30% carbon dioxide, 0%–10% oxygen, and 0%–10% methane.

70. The Chinese Shar-Pei was bred to be a fighting dog, and the loose skin was so that its opponent couldn't bite down directly onto its body.

71. The fire-breathing triceratops in Super Mario is named *Reznor* and is named after the Nine Inch Nails frontman Trent Reznor.

72. The first vibrator was invented in the late 1850s as a home treatment for "Female Hysteria".

73. The flag of Denmark has been in use since the 1300s — with a banner featuring its white-on-red cross attested to having been used by the kings of Denmark since the 14th century.

74.   The largest butterfly in the world is the Queen Alexandra's birdwing, with females reaching wingspans slightly in excess of 25 cm (9.8 inches).

75.   The late actor and martial artist Bruce Lee was also a champion ballroom dancer.

76.   The Maine coon cat breed is also known as the pirate cat, and were kept on ships to deal with rodents.

77.   The mayor of Talkeetna in Alaska was a cat named Stubbs, from 1997 until his death.

78.   The national animal of Scotland is the unicorn.

79.   The novel *The Phantom of the Opera* was written in 1909 by Gaston Leroux and was not in any way a great success.

80.   The Oxford English Dictionary credits Charles Dickens with the first use of the words *butter-fingers, crossfire, dustbin, fairy story, slow-coach*, and *whoosh* (among many others).

81.   The pill bug (woodlouse) is not actually a bug — it is an isopod crustacean.

82.   The raffia palm has the longest leaves of any tree, growing up to 25 m (82 ft.) long.

83.   The term *pit bull* refers to a number of 'dangerous' dog breeds, including the American pit bull terrier as well as the Staffordshire terrier.

84.   The *Tetris* tune is actually a 150-year-old Russian folk song.

85.   The U.S. Navy uses dolphins and sea lions to help locate underwater mines.

86.   The urine of the Southeast Asia bearcat smells like buttered popcorn because of the

chemical compound 2-AP — the same substance that gives fresh popcorn its yummy smell.

87. The video game *Minecraft* was sold to Microsoft in 2015 for $2.5 billion USD.

88. There is a place in Africa where the Namib desert meets the sea.

89. There is no lead in a pencil.

90. Time seems to pass more slowly for lighter animals with faster metabolisms.

91. To date, Adam Rainer is the only person in medical history to have been classified both as a dwarf and a giant.

92. U.S. president Richard Nixon could play the piano, saxophone, clarinet, accordion, and violin.

93.   Until 1903, Coca-Cola contained cocaine as a regular ingredient.

94.   Upon reaching adulthood, the male *flabby whalefish* fuses its mouth shut and stops feeding. It loses its stomach and esophagus and uses energy from previous meals to grow a massive liver which supports the fish for life.

95.   Vincent Castiglia is an American artist who paints exclusively with human blood.

96.   Wes Anderson's film, *Fantastic Mr. Fox*, used 535 stop-motion animation puppets.

97.   When Charles Dickens gave his first public reading in America, the line of people in New York City queuing for tickets was almost a mile long.

98.   When submerged in water, a can of diet Coca-Cola will float but a normal can of Coca-Cola will sink.

99.   You can be allergic to exercise.

100. Your capacity for kindness and empathy is predetermined by your DNA. A certain gene produces a receptor for oxytocin, the 'love hormone'. The receptor determines how much compassion you are inclined to show toward others.

Section Two:
101–200

101-200

101. "Pneumonoultramicroscopicsilicovolcan oconiosis" is the longest word in the English language and is a kind of lung disease.

102. 2016 was the hottest year ever recorded, with 16 of the 17 warmest years having occurred since 2000.

103. A 454 kg (1,000 lb.) horse produces up to 23 kg (51 lbs.) of manure per day.

104. A Hong Kong gangster once kidnapped the son of Asia's richest man and extracted a $130 million USD ransom for him. The gangster

later telephoned the tycoon father and asked for advice on how best to invest it.

105. A woman crashed her own funeral after her husband hired hitmen to kill her. They let her go, telling her they didn't believe in killing women. Five days later she appeared at her own funeral with her husband pleading for forgiveness.

106. According to the Geneva Convention, playing dead in order to kill or capture the enemy is a war crime.

107. Amish children only go to school until the eighth grade.

108. Annie Edson Taylor was the first woman to go over Niagara Falls in a barrel and survive.

109. Annie Hawkins-Turner holds the Guinness World Record for the largest natural (unenhanced) breasts — with an under-breast measurement of 109.22 cm (43 in) and an around-chest-over-nipple measurement of 177.8 cm (70 in).

110. *Anosmia* is a condition where you completely lose your sense of smell.

111. Baby koalas eat a liquefied form of their mother's feces to give them the needed microbes to digest toxins found in eucalyptus leaves.

112. Budgies (parakeets) in the wild sleep upside down so they can easily escape predators.

113. Carl Sagan, the American astronomer, cosmologist, astrophysicist, astrobiologist,

author, and science popularizer, was really rather quite fond of smoking pot.

114. Clamping your nose and closing your mouth while sneezing can damage your eardrums and sinuses.

115. Coby the blue-eyed cat has over 1.1 million followers on Instagram as of August 2017.

116. Coca-Cola will pay $1,000,000 USD to anyone who can find a new source of natural sweetener.

117. Costco stores are deliberately designed without signs, so people are forced to wander the store and buy more.

118. *Dermatoglyphics* and *uncopyrightable* are the only 2 fifteen-letter words that do not repeat a letter.

119. Ethan Zuckerman, the man responsible for inventing pop-up ads, has apologized to the world for creating one of the internet's most hated forms of advertising.

120. Every time you sneeze, your heart stops for a fraction of a second.

121. Female kangaroos have three vaginas.

122. *Fregoli delusion* is the belief that everyone you meet is the same person in disguise.

123. German fashion designer Anke Domaske creates clothing out of sour milk. No one quite knows why.

124. Google receives more than 2 million job applications per year.

125. Hans Asperger identified autism in 1944.

126. *Hypnophobia* is the fear of falling asleep.

127. Iceland is very protective of their language and doesn't borrow words from English.

128. Immigrants have a higher risk of developing schizophrenia due to the increased amount of dopamine released when migrating to a new country.

129. In 1916, the German Empire allowed citizens to take passport photos with their dogs.

130. In 2011, a Brazilian man found a penguin, covered in oil and close to death. He nursed him back to health and since then the penguin swims 8,000 km every year to see the man.

131. In 2015 alone, Netflix members streamed 42.5 billion hours of programming.

132. In 2016, KFC released a scented candle that had the smell of fried chicken.

133. In 2017, Google will reach 100% renewable energy for all their global operations.

134. In a 2009 survey, when British children under the age of 10 were asked who the most famous person in the world was, they placed the Queen third, God second, and Simon Cowell first.

135. In roughly 21% of identical twins, one is left-handed and the other right-handed or ambidextrous.

136. In some countries, blowing smoke in someone's face can be libel for a case of assault and battery.

137.   In Szymbark, Poland, is a house that was built upside-down and stands on its roof.

138.   In the Czech Republic, there is no Santa Clause. The children believe that Baby Jesus brings them the Christmas gifts.

139.   In the film *How the Grinch Stole Christmas*, Jim Carrey's Grinch suit was covered in yak hairs that were dyed green.

140.   In the U.S. state of Florida, the prison's executioner is paid $150 dollars USD per execution and is an anonymous private citizen.

141.   In the U.S. state of Kentucky, there was a family, the Fugates, which had blue blood and blue skin.

142.   In was illegal for anyone in the United States to possess gold from 1933 to 1974.

143. It has been scientifically proven that alcohol increases creativity.

144. It is a rule of the New York Mafia families that they are not allowed to grow facial hair.

145. It is possible to get cancer of the heart, but it is very rare.

146. Las Vegas, Nevada, is currently the only city in the world to rely only on green energy to power its municipal facilities.

147. Less than 30% of China's airspace can be used by commercial airlines.

148. Male host sharks have a retractable sex organ on their foreheads.

149. Mandarin, Hungarian, and Finnish are among the most difficult languages for non-natives to learn.

150. Melania Trump is the second First Lady not born in the USA.

151. Nearly 2.7 million animals are euthanized per year in the USA alone.

152. Only in 2011 did Russia acknowledge beer as alcohol. Prior to this, it was considered a soft drink because it contained less than 10% alcohol.

153. Poison dart frogs will lose their toxicity while kept in captivity.

154. Pope Francis has only one lung. One of his lungs was removed when he was a teenager due to infection.

155. *Remembrance of Things Past,* written by Marcel Proust, is 9,609,000 characters long and is the longest novel ever written.

156.   Saturn is mostly made up of gas.

157.   Seeing a spider drop down from its web was considered very good luck in early China.

158.   Sharks are able to give virgin birth although it is very rare.

159.   Some trees have what's called "crown shyness", in which the crowns of fully stocked trees do not touch each other — forming a canopy with channel-like gaps.

160.   Stephen King sells the rights to some of his short stories for only $1 so film students can use them to make films.

161.   Teargas is made from chili pepper oil.

162.   The Amber Alert that goes out when a child goes missing is named after Amber Hagerman, who was kidnapped and murdered on January 13, 1996.

163. The ancient Chinese used natural gas for lighting as early as 500 B.C., using bamboo pipelines to transport the gas for miles.

164. The ballpoint pen is called a "biro" in England and was created by László Bíró and his brother.

165. The Beatles planned to call their 1969 album release *Everest* — an inside joke about the brand of cigarettes smoked by engineer Geoff Emerick. They had intended to shoot the cover photo at Mount Everest, but the album's name was ultimately changed to (nearby) *Abbey Road* because the band didn't want to go all the way to Mount Everest just for the cover photograph.

166. The bubbles in Guinness beer sink to the bottom instead of floating to the top.

167. The city of Holland, Michigan, has 168 miles of tubing coiled underneath its streets circulating hot water in order to melt any snow on the ground.

168. The clock tower of the Palace of Westminster is not actually called Big Ben. Big Ben is the name of its clock's bell.

169. The Collito family of Massachusetts observed an abandoned and sickly kitten in their backyard being fed and nursed back to health by a crow. The family adopted the kitten, and the kitten and the crow remain fast friends and are often seen playing together.

170. The domain name *vacationrentals.com* was bought for $35 million USD.

171. The first known photograph of the United States White House was taken in 1846 by John Plumbe Jr. — who was an immigrant from

Wales and the country's first prominent photographer.

172. The first women's boxing competition was sanctioned in 1997 by The British Amateur Boxing Association.

173. The human body produces 2.4 million red blood cells per second.

174. The invention of plastic surgery was sparked by World War I, as flying shrapnel in the war resulted in many horrific facial injuries.

175. The King of Hearts is the only king in a deck of cards without a lovely moustache.

176. The largest gingerbread man ever made was made by IKEA in Oslo Norway on November 9, 2009. It weighed 651 kg (1,435 lbs.).

177. The letter "J" is the only letter that doesn't appear on the periodic table.

178. The most expensive car ever sold was a 1963 vintage Ferrari 250 GTO which sold for $52 million USD.

179. The oldest continually inhabited city in the world is Jericho.

180. The oldest piece of music ever discovered is a 3,400-year-old cult hymn from Sumeria.

181. The record for the longest burp was 1 minute 13 seconds & 57 milliseconds and was set by Michele Forgione in June of 2009.

182. The record for the longest time spent awake was set by a high-school student in 1965, and he was awake for 11 days.

183. The Samoan moss spider holds the record as the smallest spider in the world.

184. The short-finned pilot whale and orca both go through menopause.

185. The *SIM* in sim card stands for Subscriber Identification Module.

186. The Sun is 1.392 million km (864,938 miles) in diameter.

187. The Three Gorges Dam in China is so massive it has slowed the rotation of the Earth.

188. The Tibetan mastiff became the most expensive dog breed in the world after selling for $1.9 million USD a puppy in 2014.

189. The U.S. Navy have boats called *swarm boats* that do not require a captain or, in fact, any humans aboard — they are robotic and autonomous.

190. The Ueno Zoo in Tokyo gives visitors the option to sample the food that is given to the animals.

191. The UK finished paying for WWI in 2015.

192. The voices schizophrenics hear are shaped by their local culture. Patients in America hear voices telling them to do violent things while in Africa patients usually hear the voices of dead relatives or voices offering them comfort.

193. There are over 3,500 species of mosquitoes.

194. There is an inland island in Canada that is larger in area than the lake in which it resides.

195. There is natural sugar found in tobacco, but more sugar is often added during manufacturing.

196. Thomas Edison invented what was called the "voice-driven sewing machine" — which worked by speaking into its "phonomotor" mouthpiece.

197. U.S. president William Howard Taft had an inordinate fondness for bathtubs.

198. Upon her death, as per her request, the late actress Carrie Fisher was cremated, and her ashes placed in an urn that looks like a Prozac pill.

199. Wolfgang Amadeus Mozart had an older sister, Maria Anna Mozart, who was also a child prodigy. The two performed together until she was 18.

200. WWI and II demand resulted a shortage of steel which led to some ships being built with concrete. 10 of those ships are still afloat in a small coastal town of British Columbia.

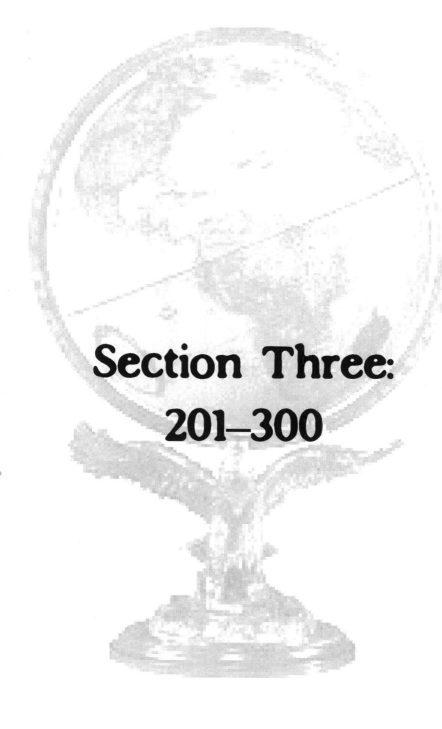

Section Three: 201–300

201-300

201. "Billy Jean" by Michael Jackson was the first music video by an African-American artist to air on MTV.

202. "Graffito" is the singular form of *graffiti*.

203. 14.5 billion electronic messages received on a daily basis are spam.

204. A flea can jump 100 times its height.

205. A killer whale's dorsal fin will go limp if the orca is kept in captivity.

206. A male kangaroo can hop up to 70 km/h (44 mph) and can jump as high as 10 feet.

207. A study has found that 1 in 5 corporate executives is a psychopath.

208. According to a poll, New Hampshire is the least-religious U.S. state.

209. According to addiction experts, giving your child a smartphone is the equivalent of giving them a gram of cocaine.

210. Adventurer Raphael Domjan has created a solar-powered airplane that is said to become the first ever to reach the stratosphere.

211. After Ozzy Osbourne left Black Sabbath, Michael Bolton auditioned to replace him.

212. Allergies to Brazil nuts can be passed on sexually.

213. Almonds were grown thousands of years ago without having an official name. It took some time before the name *almond* was created. This was because botanists kept thinking up new names for it.

214. Ancient Egyptians believed that mushrooms were the plant of immortality.

215. André the Giant holds the record for consuming the most beer in a single sitting and had held the record for the past 40 years.

216. Apollo 11 astronaut Buzz Aldrin took communion on the moon.

217. As of 2011, the Hubble Space Telescope had made over 1 million observations.

218. At Imperial College London, a violin has been developed that uses in the production of its body strands of golden silk spun by an Australian golden orb-weaver spider.

219. Bagpipes were introduced to the Scottish Isles by the Romans.

220. Breathing during Diwali (the Hindu festival of Lights) in Mumbai for one day is the equivalent of smoking two packs of cigarettes.

221. British eggs are illegal in U.S. stores because they are unwashed.

222. Burj Khalifa in Dubai, the tallest structure ever built, is 828 m (2,717 ft.) tall — so tall it pierces the clouds.

223. California's state motto is, "Eureka" (I have found it).

224. Cookie Monster from *Sesame Street's* real name is Sid.

225. Despite factors like income, living where you can see the ocean has been found to reduce psychological stress.

226. Domino's Pizza dropped their 30-minutes-or-less guarantee in 1993 after a series of lawsuits maintaining that it encouraged unsafe driving on the part of their drivers.

227. During the Age of Discovery, Portuguese soldiers used black swords so there would be no reflection of light to warn enemies of their presence.

228. Egyptian Pharaoh Tutankhamun's penis was mummified erect.

229. Electric cars are so quiet that they are required by law to produce artificial engine noise to help keep pedestrians from being taken unawares and getting hurt.

230. Flamingos can drink boiling water (though it is unclear why they should want to).

231. Giant anteaters' tongues can extend out of their mouths up to 610 mm (24 in.).

232. In 1920, Thomas Edison tried to build a "spirit phone" to contact the dead.

233. In 1979, the American TV show *The Muppets* was banned in Saudi Arabia because of its porcine character Miss Piggy.

234. In China, ground bees are used as a remedy for a sore throat.

235. In order to grow bananas, you need both a male and female banana tree (who love each other very, very much).

236. In recent years, the number of people donating their bodies to science has doubled due to high funeral costs. Schools will cremate what remains of the body and return it to the family.

237. In some Chinese subway stations, people are employed to help shove people into overly-crowded trains.

238. In the 1970s, serial killer Ted Bundy worked at a suicide hotline crisis center.

239. In the film *Fantasia*, the sorcerer's name is Yen Sid — which is 'Disney' spelled backwards.

240. James Madison, the 4th president of the United States, was the shortest president at only 5 feet 4 inches tall (163 cm).

241. Kuwait banned the 2017 film *Beauty and the Beast* due to its gay character (LeFou).

242. Lake Karachay in Russia, formerly used as a dumping site for nuclear waste, holds the distinction of being the most polluted place on earth.

243. Lottery winner Jack Whittaker was once robbed of $545,000 in cash. When asked why he carried around that much money, he replied by saying, "Because I can."

244. Marie Curie was the first woman to receive a PhD from a French university and the first woman to be employed as a scientist. She was also the first person to win the Nobel Prize award twice for two distinct scientific fields.

245. Most species of gecko, as a defense mechanism, will shed their tails if tugged.

246. Mr. T wore gold chains he collected while working as a bouncer. They were either lost or left behind by customers after fights.

247. *Mythbusters* had planned to do an episode which highlighted the immense security flaws in most credit cards, but the Discovery Channel was threatened by, and eventually gave in to, immense legal pressure from the major credit card companies.

248. New Zealand has two national anthems — "God Defend New Zealand" and "God Save the Queen."

249. Of the tens of thousands of deaths occurring annually due to rabies, 95% of cases are reported in Asia and Africa.

250. On June 27, 2016, Norway held the biggest bonfire ever— which measured 47.4 m (155.5 ft.) tall.

251. Our memories are so easy to manipulate that in 3 hours you can believe you committed a crime that never happened. Researchers were able to convince 70% of study participants they were guilty of a fake crime — to which they confessed, and to which they also gave detailed descriptions of.

252. Peanuts can be used in the production of dynamite.

253. Pistol shrimp have a punch that is faster than a .22-caliber bullet.

254. Scientists at the University of Nottingham hold the record for writing the world's smallest periodic table — engraved on a strand of hair.

255. Some species of salamander have no lungs and survive by breathing through their skin.

256. Superman's creators Jerry Siegel and Joe Shuster sold the rights to their character to DC Comics in 1938 for $130 (split between them).

257. The "Big Bang" theory, as it came to be known, was first proposed by Georges Lemaître — a Catholic priest.

258. The "Underwear Bomber" plot failed because the bomber, Umar Abdulmutallab, wore the same underwear for 2 weeks straight, and as a result, the bomb's fuse became "damp."

259. The average length of an umbilical cord is 52 cm (20.5 in.).

260. The bald eagle can live for up to 50 years.

261. The dot above an "i" is called a *tittle* and the cross on a "t" is called a *jot*.

262. The Empire State Building is hit by lighting on average 23 times a year.

263. The first letter ever rolled on the show *Wheel of Fortune* was the letter "T".

264. The first sewing needles were made of bone.

265. The first video game was invented in 1958 — a very simple tennis game, similar to the classic 1970s video game *Pong*.

266. The first words Russian President Boris Yeltsin said to U.S. President Clinton upon meeting in 1995 were, "Do you think O.J. did it?"

267. The founder of BMW, Günther Quandt, was a member of the Nazi party and supplied the regime with ammunition.

268. The French bulldog originated in England.

269. The giant Gippsland earthworm of Australia average 1 m (3.3 ft.) long and 2 cm (0.79 in) in diameter and can reach 3 meters (9.8 ft.) in length.

270. The Huns could not write, and all their depictions were written by their enemies.

271. The inventor of the 5-hour ENERGY™ drink was a monk for 12 years.

272. The largest cells that exist in nature are (unfertilized) ostrich eggs.

273. The largest snail ever found weighed 2 pounds and measured 15.5 inches from snout to tail.

274. The largest solar plant in the world is located in the Mohave Desert.

275. The longest human excrement ever recorded was an astonishing 7.92 m (26 ft.) and was set in 1995 — by a woman.

276. The melody for the American National Anthem is based on an old English drinking song.

277. The Milky Way is about 100,000 light years across.

278. The Nathan Bedford Forrest High School in Jacksonville, Florida, is named after the first "Grand Wizard" of the KKK.

279. The odorous house ant smells like rotten coconut when crushed.

280. The only capital city in the world which doesn't have traffic lights is Bhutan in the Himalayas.

281. The only known herbivorous spider is the *Bagheera kiplingi* spider.

282. The original lyrics for Little Richard's song "Tutti Frutti" were changed from "Tutti frutti, loose booty" to "Tutti frutti, aw Rooty" because the original was considered scandalous.

283. The Pony Express was only in operation for 2 years.

284. The Pringles cartoon mascot man's name is Julius.

285. The Republic of Madagascar is the 4th-largest island in the world.

286. The *Sobrino de Botin* is officially recognized as the world's oldest continuously-in-use restaurant and was founded in 1725.

287. The Suriname toad gives birth through holes in its back.

288. The United States uses 25% of the world's natural resources, and produces 30% of the world's waste.

289. The widest human mouth was measured in 2010 at 17 cm (6.7 in.).

290. The word "testify" comes from the Latin world for testicle.

291. The world's largest single-celled organism is an alga called *Caulerpa taxifolia*, and grows as large as 12 inches (30.5 cm).

292. Theo Albrecht, co-founder of the discount store Aldi, negotiated his own ransom when he was kidnapped and held for 17 days. He later won tax relief on the ransom payment, claiming it was a business expense.

293. There are 'tornados' of plasma on the surface of the Sun.

294. There are more microorganisms in a teaspoon of healthy soil than there are people on Earth.

295. There is a city in Russia so contaminated with nuclear waste that before buying food, people must have all items checked with a Geiger counter.

296. Toronto, Ontario, Canada, hosts over 75 film festivals every year.

297. U.S. President Abraham Lincoln's VP, Andrew Johnson, was drunk on whiskey while taking his oath of office.

298. Uranus is the only planet that rotates on its side.

299. Vampire bats urinate on whatever animal they are drinking from.

300. Venice, Italy, sinks about 1 to 2 mm a year and is slowly tilting to the east.

Section Four:
301–400

301-400

301. "Run" has 645 different meanings in English —and that's just in its verb form.

302. 100 people choke to death on a ballpoint pen cap each year (the number used to be higher before holes at the tip of the caps were introduced).

303. 400 million years ago, mushrooms grew tall — taller than a giraffe.

304. 7 pitches is the average lifespan of a Major League baseball.

305. A "jiffy" is an actual measure of time — 1/100th of a second.

306. A 42-year-old Russian was viciously attacked by a bear, but he was suddenly saved when the ringtone his granddaughter installed on his mobile phone went off, and Justin Bieber's "Baby" sent the bear running in distress back to the woods.

307. A horseshoe crab's copper-based blood is blue.

308. A hungry wolf can eat 20 pounds of meat in a single meal, which is equivalent to a human eating 100 hamburgers in one sitting.

309. A London woman developed Permanent Sexual Arousal Syndrome (PSAS) at age 19 and now has as many as 200 orgasms a day.

310. A palm tree isn't really a tree; it's a type of grass.

311. A person falls asleep in, on average, 7 minutes.

312. A toxic dose of ground nutmeg is 2 to 3 teaspoons.

313. Abu Dhabi has a beauty contest for camels.

314. Adam West (born 1928) was 11 years older than Batman (created 1939).

315. Agatha Christie's book *Ten Little Indians* was called *Ten Little Niggers* when it was originally published in 1939.

316. Alaska has the highest percentage of people who walk to work of any U.S. state.

317. Ambergris, colloquially known as "whale vomit" and a rare but valuable find on beaches, is worth nearly its weight in gold.

318. An eagle can fly while carrying a young deer.

319. Angel Falls (Salto Ángel) in Venezuela is the highest waterfall in the world. The falls are 3,230 feet in height.

320. As of 2010, Bill Gates has donated over half of his estate to charity.

321. Bill Murray agreed to voice Garfield in the live action movie because he thought the film was being written by one of the Coen Brothers (of *Fargo, The Big Lebowski*, etc.).

322. Brass doorknobs disinfect themselves after 8 hours. It's called the oligodynamic effect.

323. Butterflies taste with their feet.

324. By 2014, "Gangnam Style" had been collectively watched the equivalent of 15,400 years.

325. *Continuum* was a magazine that denied the existence of HIV/AIDS. It stopped publication in 2001 after all its editorial staff died of AIDS.

326. Currently, American pro baseball players make an average of $4.25 million a year.

327. Currently, the oldest authenticated age any human has lived is 122 years 164 days — by Jeanne Louise Calment (France).

328. Dolphins can help overcome sleep deprivation and remain constantly vigilant for days at a time by resting one half of their brain while the other half remains conscious.

329. Dora the Explorer's real name is Dora Márquez.

330. Drinking too much water (water intoxication) can kill you.

331. Due to radiation from the Sun, all the U.S. flags on the Moon are now white.

332. Due to the shortage of metal during WWII, the Oscars trophies were made of painted plaster.

333. Everyone's tongue print is unique.

334. Everything you're experiencing right now actually happened 80 milliseconds ago.

335. Gambling dens in the 18th century employed someone to swallow the dice if there was a police raid.

336. Graveyards and cemeteries are not the same thing — a graveyard is always connected to a church, but a cemetery is not. Also, you are allowed to bury ashes in a cemetery.

337. Having red hair and blue eyes is the rarest combination in the world.

338. Horses can't vomit.

339. In 1975, Charlie Chaplin entered a Charlie Chaplin look-alike contest — and came in third.

340. In 2011, a 75-year-old woman sliced through a fiber-optic cable, cutting 2 entire countries off the internet.

341. In licking a stamp, you consume 1/10th of a calorie.

342. It is possible for the kangaroo rat to live its entire life without drinking water.

343. John Glenn, the lst American to orbit Earth, spotted a cloud of strange "fireflies" on his 2nd orbit. Later, NASA confirmed that the 'fireflies' were simply droplets of Glenn's own urine that had been expelled from his craft during the previous orbit.

344. Kangaroos cannot walk (or jump, as the case may be) backwards. Also, if a kangaroo's tail is lifted off of the ground, they can't hop.

345. Lake Baikal, in Siberia, is the deepest lake on Earth with a maximum depth of 1,642 m (5,387 ft.), and holds over 20% of the Earth's surface freshwater.

346. Lake Superior has enough water to flood the entire landmasses of North and South America under a foot of water.

347. McDonald's drive-thru staff aren't allowed to serve people on horseback.

348. Men, generally speaking, are able to read smaller print than woman.

349. Most lipstick contains fish scales.

350. "Mr Poo" is a mascot in India that discourages people from defecating in public.

351. Nearly all koala bears have chlamydia.

352. Night-running is a traditional activity in Kenya where people run naked at night.

353. On Venus, it snows metal.

354. One of the early products developed by the Galvin Manufacturing Corp was the car radio, in 1930. Its popularity prompted the

company to change its name to Motorola — hence the "motor" in Motorola.

355. Only female mosquitoes bite (males feed on flower nectar).

356. Opossums can pass out from extreme fear — and do so as a bizarre defense mechanism.

357. Over 75,000 Americans are awaiting organ transplants.

358. Oxford University is older than the Aztec Empire.

359. Penguins can jump up out of the water nearly 10 feet.

360. People with blue eyes have one common ancestor who appeared 6,000–10,000 years ago.

361. Roughly 15 tons of soil per acre pass through one earthworm each year, and 1,400,000 earthworms can be found in one acre of cropland.

362. Should the U.S. president's wife die while he is in office, one of his female relatives becomes the First Lady.

363. Sneezing too hard can fracture your ribs.

364. Sunflowers can be used in cleaning up nuclear waste.

365. The book holding the record for the most-often stolen from libraries is the *Guinness Book of World Records*.

366. The Catholic Church once put a dead Pope on trial. He lost, and was retroactively un-poped.

367. The Church of Satan neither believes in nor worships Satan.

368. The *Cotard delusion*, known colloquially as the "Walking Dead Syndrome", is a psychological disorder in which a sufferer believes they are dead.

369. The hydrogen bomb RDS22 ("Tsar Bomba") was the most powerful nuclear weapon ever detonated. Its test on 30 October 1961 remains the most powerful man-made explosion in history.

370. The *International Space Station* is the most expensive institution ever built — costing $150 billion USD.

371. The lead singer of the metal band Hatebeak is a Congo African grey parrot.

372. The leg bones of bats are so thin and fragile that most bats can't walk, and use their legs only for hanging.

373. The Lorillard Tobacco Company (now defunct) was the oldest continuously-running tobacco company in the U.S. — from 1760–2005.

374. The modern-day bulletproof vest was invented by a woman — Stephanie Kwolek, working at DuPont, who developed Kevlar®.

375. The Moon moves away from the Earth at a tiny rate each year.

376. The movie *Fuck* (2005 documentary) holds the record for the most times the word is used in a film — 824.

377. The music for *Sonic 3: Project Chaos* was, in part, composed by Michael Jackson.

378. The novel *Tom Sawyer* was the first to be written on a typewriter, according to its author Mark Twain.

379. The oldest tree on Earth is nearly 5,000 years old—about as old as the pyramids of Egypt.

380. The phrase "luck of the Irish" was originally meant as an insult, and had an ironic and negative connotation.

381. The science of kissing is called *philematology*.

382. The smell of fresh-cut grass is as a result of a chemical distress call.

383. The space between your eyebrows is called the *glabella*.

384. The Statue of Liberty is made out of copper. When originally built, it looked like a shiny new penny.

385. The traditional "last meal" for those condemned to death didn't begin as a final compassionate act for them but, rather, as a way to bribe their ghost not to haunt the executioners.

386. The United States experiences 75% of the world's tornados.

387. The very first Ronald McDonald was portrayed by a weatherman named Willard Scott.

388. The word *utopia* comes from a Greek word which means "no place".

389. There is a desk in the U.S. Senate Chamber always filled with candy.

390. Three books in the Harvard University library are bound in human flesh.

391. Trailers are called that because, originally, they used to be shown at the end of the movie — trailing the film.

392. Two rats in an ideal environment can turn into 482 million rats over a period of three years.

393. Undertaker bees remove the bodies of dead bees and carry them away from the hive.

394. When dropped into a glass of champagne, a raisin will continuously float up and down.

395. When properly sealed in containers, honey will stay edible for thousands of years.

396. Winds on Uranus and Neptune can reach supersonic speeds.

397. With the energy saved from recycling one aluminum can, you can power a TV for three hours.

398. You can pay to go with National Geographic on its expeditions to exotic places, such as Antarctica.

399. You can't cry in space because there is no gravity — your eyes make tears, but they stick there as a liquid ball and don't flow.

400. Your heart beats about 100,000 times a day.

Section Five:
401–500

401-500

401. "Go" is the shortest complete sentence in the English language.

402. 1 in every 5 adults believes aliens hide on the planet in human form, according to respondents polled from a 2010 Reuters global survey.

403. 10% of the world's population is left-handed.

404. A Canadian man who was freed in 2017 after being held in Afghanistan by Taliban-tied kidnappers for 5 years said he was certain his

captors were joking when they told him Donald Trump was president.

405. A concealed room under the Medici Chapel is covered in charcoal sketches by Michelangelo, who lived there for 3 months while hiding from the Pope.

406. A coyote can hear a mouse moving under a foot of snow.

407. A pig's orgasm can last up to 30 minutes.

408. A *sapiosexual* is a person who is sexually attracted to intelligence in others.

409. A single cloud weighs an average of 1.1 million pounds (500,000 kg).

410. After mating, the male bee's testicles explode and the bee dies.

411.   Al Capone's business card said he was a used furniture dealer.

412.   Albert Einstein's last words were spoken in German to a nurse who *könnte nicht deutsch sprechen*, and thus are forever lost to posterity.

413.   *All Quiet on the Western Front* was banned in Poland for being pro-German and in Germany for being anti-German.

414.   As you read this, Earth will have travelled more than 5,000 miles in the past 5 minutes.

415.   Benjamin Franklin left the cities of Boston and Philadelphia $2,000 in his will, but they could not draw the full balance for 200 years. In 1990, the cities received a total of $6.5 million.

416. Bob Marley's last words (which were to his son, Ziggy) were, "Money can't buy life."

417. Collectively, humans have watched Adam Sandler movies on Netflix for longer than civilization has existed.

418. *Dendrophilia* is the sexual arousal from trees.

419. Dolphins go on killing sprees when they're sexually frustrated.

420. Dolphins tenderize octopuses by bashing them about before consuming them.

421. Ethiopia has a space program.

422. Even after extinction, the dodo is still the national animal of Mauritius.

423. Farmers in Botswana have started painting eyes on their cattle's rumps to prevent lion attacks — hoping to trick the big cats, who prefer stealth kills, into thinking they have been seen.

424. Gangster John Dillinger reportedly once escaped from prison by carving a potato into the shape of a pistol. Sources do not reveal, however, if the potato-pistol was fully functional.

425. George Washington spent an estimated 7% of his presidential salary on alcohol.

426. Goats have rectangular pupils.

427. Hong Kong has the most Rolls-Royce (and Mercedes) cars per capita.

428. Human birth-control pills also work for use in gorillas.

429. Hummingbirds are the only bird species that can hover, and fly backwards, or even upside down.

430. Iceland imports ice cubes.

431. In 1,500 B.C., a shaved head was considered the ultimate beauty in Egypt.

432. In 1386, a pig in France was executed by public hanging for the murder of a child. It was given full legal representation and provided human clothing for trial.

433. In 1859, a moral panic swept America over young people playing entirely too much chess.

434. In 1880s England, the word "pants" was considered a word unutterable in polite company.

435. In 2008, a British 19-year-old officially changed his name to "Captain Fantastic Faster Than Superman Spiderman Batman Wolverine Hulk And The Flash Combined." He was a very silly person indeed.

436. In 2009, Canada passed the "Apology Act", stating that apologizing to someone after an incident cannot be used in court against the person who apologized to establish their guilt or liability.

437. In 2012, a cat named Orlando beat top investment bankers in a year-long investment competition, which he chose by throwing his favorite mouse toy at a grid to select companies to invest in.

438. In 2015, two con men sold a fake Goya painting for €1.5 million ($1.74 million USD), only to find out that all the money they received for it was counterfeit.

439. In competitive shooting, alcohol is considered a performance-enhancing drug and, as such, is banned.

440. In Japan, there are cafés where you can consort with owls.

441. In Russia, mail carriers carry revolvers.

442. In Sweden, you can buy toilet paper called *Kräpp*.

443. In the 18th century, tobacco was used for "rectal inflation" — blowing smoke up the anus to resuscitate the drowned.

444. In the 1930s, tomato ketchup was used as medicine.

445. In the U.S. in 1998, more fast-food restaurant workers were killed on the job than were police officers.

446. In Turkey during the 16th and 17th century, anyone drinking coffee was put to death.

447. James Buchanan, the 15th President of the U.S., bought slaves with his own money in order to free them.

448. Leonardo da Vinci was an accomplished lyre player. When he was first presented at the Milanese court, it was as a musician rather than an artist or inventor.

449. Lightning kills 6 times more men than women.

450. Most people in the 18th century only had a proper wash twice a year.

451. New York drifts away from London at the rate of 1 inch (2.5 cm) per year — and Hawaii is

moving 4 inches (10 cm) closer to Japan each year.

452. On a 1995 visit to Washington D.C., Russian President Boris Yeltsin was found on Pennsylvania Avenue, drunk, in his underwear, trying to hail a cab to get a pizza.

453. On average, the typical American will drink 238 cans of soda per year.

454. On Father's Day, there are more collect calls made than any other day of the year.

455. One of Richard Nixon's re-election slogans in 1972 was "They Can't Lick our Dick."

456. Only men were allowed to eat at the first self-service cafeteria-style restaurant, the Exchange Buffet.

457. Pieces of bread, among other things, were used to erase pencil markings before rubber came into use.

458. Pope Benedict IX was the youngest in history, becoming pope at perhaps 11 years old (exact age uncertain).

459. Russia has 800,000 faith healers but only 640,000 doctors.

460. Shakespeare spelled his own name several different ways.

461. Similar to "fake news", the *Lügenpresse* accusation was used by the Nazis to discredit unsupportive media outlets.

462. Some of the bears in Russia are addicted to huffing jet fuel fumes due to the discarded gasoline and kerosene containers in the Far East.

463. Sometimes Moscow's ultra-rich drive around in ambulances so they can get around the typically horrendous traffic.

464. Sony makes more money as an insurance company in Japan than selling electronics.

465. The "Groom of the Stool" was perhaps the most familiar of an English monarch's attendants, responsible for assisting the King in excretion and ablution.

466. The act of chewing gum burns roughly 11 calories per hour.

467. The average pencil holds enough graphite to draw a line about 35 miles (56 km) long.

468. The average person throughout their lifetime spends roughly six months of that in waiting at traffic lights.

469. The blobfish (of internet fame) actually looks as normal as any other fish. It just decompresses when it's taken out of the extreme depths in which it lives.

470. The distinctive green falling code in *The Matrix* film is just lots and lots of Japanese sushi recipes.

471. The electric chair was invented by a dentist — Alfred P. Southwick from Buffalo, New York.

472. The first Fords had engines made by Dodge.

473. The horseshoe crab has eyes (photo receptors) on its tail.

474. The Japanese embassy in France has a 24-hour helpline for their citizens who didn't find Paris quite as delightful as expected.

475. The oldest piece of chewing gum ever found is thought to be 9,000 years old.

476. The only woman in Einstein's physics class at Zürich Polytechnic married him.

477. The original patent for the toilet-roll holder showed the paper — quite sensibly — hanging *over* the holder and not under.

478. The position your body is in can affect your memory.

479. The Queen of England is related to Vlad the Impaler.

480. The Sun is about 400 times farther from Earth than the Moon — and because Earth's moon is 400 times smaller than the Sun, the Sun and Moon appear nearly the same size as seen from Earth during a solar eclipse.

481. The *Turritopsis dohrnii* is a species of jellyfish that is essentially immortal.

482. The world's largest pizza was about 2.5 times as big as a basketball court. That's *gigantesco*.

483. The youngest mother in recorded history was Peruvian Lina Medina — who gave birth to a baby boy at the age of 5 in 1939.

484. *Theinism* is chronic poisoning resulting from immoderate levels of tea-drinking.

485. There is a deep-sea fish called the Atlantic wolffish which produces its own antifreeze to keep the blood flowing.

486. There is a garbage swirl in the Pacific Ocean — The Great Pacific garbage patch, also described as the *Pacific trash vortex* — that is roughly the size of Texas.

487. There is more gold dissolved in the Earth's oceans than has been mined throughout all of human history.

488. Though much younger historically, the U.S. is an older country than Germany — which became a nation in 1871 when most of the German states unified.

489. Throughout a lifetime, the average person will walk the equivalent of 5 times around the Earth.

490. To visit every child in the world, Santa Claus needs to travel at 3,000 times the speed of sound.

491. Toto the dog (real name Terry) was paid $125 per week while filming *The Wizard of Oz* — more than that of many human actors in the film.

492. U.S. President George W. Bush named *The Very Hungry Caterpillar* by Eric Carle as his favorite childhood book. It was published when he was 23 years old.

493. Volkswagen sold more sausages than cars in 2015.

494. Wal-Mart is the single largest employer in 20 U.S. states.

495. Western Union didn't stop sending telegrams until 2006.

496. When a North Korean merchant vessel was attacked by Somali pirates in 2007, an American destroyer came to their aid. This event led to rare pro-U.S. statements from the North Korean media.

497. When anglerfish mate, the male latches onto the female's body and fuses to her, losing

all his internal organs, until they share a bloodstream.

498. When hunting is good and a polar bear's body is in good condition, the bear may eat only the seal's blubber and skin.

499. When the first McDonald's drive-through in Kuwait opened, the queue was 7 miles long.

500. You can buy a toupée for your dog in Tokyo (from a vending machine, no less).

Section Six:
501–600

501-600

501. *Colgate* — when spoken in certain Spanish dialects — translates to "go hang yourself."

502. 10,000 foxes live in London.

503. 98% of adoptions in Japan are adult adoptions — mostly men 20–30 years old.

504. A "non-visible" piece of art was purchased in 2011 for $10,000 USD.

505. A ball of glass will bounce higher than a ball of rubber.

506. A Chinese gamer died in 2005 of fatigue after playing *World of Warcraft* for 3 days straight.

507. A cockroach can live for several weeks after its head has been removed from its body.

508. A mantis shrimp can swing its claw so fast that it boils the surrounding water and causes a flash of light.

509. A quarter of all the bones in the human body are located in a person's feet.

510. A sheep, a rooster, and a duck were the first passengers on a hot air balloon.

511. All astronauts must learn how to speak Russian, and all cosmonauts must learn how to speak English.

512. An aversion to happiness is called *cherophobia*.

513. An ostrich's eye is bigger than its brain.

514. Ancient Greeks wouldn't eat beans as they thought they contained the souls of the dead.

515. Anyone over 14 can drive a VSP (*voiture sans permis*) car in France without a license.

516. As a child, Adolf Hitler wanted to be a priest.

517. Author Ray Bradbury was so poor growing up that he borrowed the suit with a bullet hole his uncle was murdered in for his high school graduation ceremony.

518. Avocados are poisonous to birds (which means more guacamole for us).

519. Babies are born with 300 bones (compared to the 206 found in adults).

520. Beetles taste like apples.

521. Birds don't urinate.

522. Brazil holds an annual *Miss BumBum* pageant to select the Brazilian woman with the most preeminent posterior.

523. British researchers have found that taking a hot bath can actually burn as many calories as a 30-minute walk.

524. Buying or selling chewing gum in Singapore is illegal.

525. Cats have 32 individual muscles in each ear.

526. Certain species of tarantula can live without food for more than 2 years.

527. China censors the word *censorship*.

528. Cows kill more people than sharks do.

529. Crete has 40 million olive trees — around 60 per inhabitant.

530. *Diphylleia grayi* is known as a "skeleton flower" because its white petals go transparent when wet, but return to white when dry.

531. Dogs are capable of doing simple mathematical calculations.

532. Dogs can understand up to 250 words and hand gestures.

533. Dogs mark their territory with urine, so they lift their legs when they do so in an effort to mark higher, making themselves appear taller (and thus more intimidating).

534. Dolphins intentionally chew on toxic pufferfish to get high.

535. Dr. Seuss had an affair while his wife suffered from cancer and depression. A few months after his wife's suicide, he married his mistress.

536. During the writers' strike in 2007, David Letterman paid writing staff of *The Late Show* out of his own pocket.

537. Earth is the only planet in our solar system not named after a Roman god or goddess.

538. For every human on Earth, there are about 1.6 million ants.

539. Golden poison dart frogs (Phyllobates terribilis) harbor enough poison to kill 10 grown men, making these frogs perhaps the most poisonous animals alive.

540. Google Earth is banned in Bahrain.

541. Gorillas belch to convey that they are not aggressive or a threat to others.

542. Houses in Bermuda produce their own water by way of rain-catching roofs — essential, as Bermuda has no fresh-water springs, rivers, or lakes.

543. Hummingbirds can weigh less than a penny.

544. If the water in your body is reduced by 12–20%, you will die. (Stay hydrated, folks!)

545. If you were to start with a single penny and double that every day, you will be a millionaire in 27 days.

546. In 1986, Apple launched a clothing line.

547. In 2014, a massive underground multi-level city, Derinkuyu, was discovered in Turkey — large enough to have sheltered as many as 20,000 people together with their livestock and food stores.

548. In an emergency, coconut water may be given intravenously in place of blood plasma.

549. In Japan, crooked teeth (yaeba (八重歯)) are considered beautiful.

550. In Japan, it is considered good fortune when a sumo wrestler makes your baby cry.

551. In May 2006, a man from Brisbane, Australia, attempted to sell New Zealand via eBay. He was unsuccessful.

552. In rare instances, gases created during the decomposition of a dead body have enough pressure to cause a dead pregnant woman to expel the fetus. It's called a "coffin birth".

553. In the U.S. state of Maryland, the official sport is jousting.

554. In the U.S., in 2016, an estimated 4.6 billion animals were slaughtered for food.

555. It is illegal in New York to sell a 'haunted' house without informing the potential buyer.

556. It is possible for a man to fracture his penis.

557. It takes 2 million flower visits for bees to produce a single pound of honey.

558. It takes about 3,000 cow hides to supply the NFL with leather for footballs each year.

559. Italian banks accept wheels of delicious Parmigiano-Reggiano cheese as collateral for loans.

560. Japan's Parasitological Museum is the world's only museum fully dedicated to parasites — hosting a collection of over 45,000 items.

561. *Kummerspeck* ("grief bacon") is German for the weight put on from eating too much when feeling sorry for yourself.

562. Las Vegas casinos have no visible clocks (and no windows).

563. Long before her featured role in *American Horror Story: Hotel*, a 15-year-old Lady GaGa appeared in Season 3 of *The Sopranos*.

564. Male ostrich can roar like lions (or make a noise, at least, that sounds remarkably like a lion's roar).

565. Mountain lions can whistle (or, at least, make a vocalization that sounds very much like a whistle).

566. Mozart kept a diary of every incident in which he heard someone fart.

567. Norway has no legal minimum wage (nor does Sweden, Denmark, Iceland, or Switzerland).

568. People with blue eyes have a higher tolerance to alcohol.

569. Pretty much anything that melts can be made into glass.

570. Prostitutes in the Netherlands pay taxes.

571. Russia has about the same surface area as Pluto.

572. Saddam Hussein was the author of a romance novel called *Zabibah and the King.*

573. Scientists believe that on Jupiter and Saturn, it rains diamonds.

574. *Special orientation phenomenon* is a rare brain condition which causes you to see everything upside down.

575. The average intelligence of humans has risen 20 IQ points since 1950, a study found.

576. The average mouth produces over 25,000 qts. (23,659 L) of saliva over a lifetime.

577. The boomslang (Dispholidus typus) snake's venom will cause you to bleed from every orifice.

578. The drummer from Def Leppard only has one arm.

579. The giant red spot on Jupiter is a storm that has been raging for over 150 years — and is larger in diameter than Earth.

580. The kakapo parrot of New Zealand is critically endangered because it has a strong and very pleasant scent that leads predators straight to it.

581. The Labrador retriever has been the most popular dog in America for the past 26 years, according to the American Kennel Club.

582. The longest engagement on record was between Octavio Guillan and Adriana Martjnez. They finally tied the knot after 67 years in June 1969 in Mexico City.

583. The Spanish national anthem has no words.

584. The woman who made cannabis brownies famous by baking and distributing them to AIDS patients was named Mary Jane (Mary Jane Rathbun).

585. The woolly mammoth was still around when the pyramids were being built.

586. The word "set" has the most definitions of any word in the English language (464).

587. The word *gorilla* is derived from the Greek word meaning "tribe of hairy women".

588. There are 173 known moons in our solar system.

589. There are 5 temples in Kyoto, Japan, that have blood-stained ceilings.

590. There is a restaurant in Taiwan which serves your food on a miniature toilet.

591. There is a shrub (*Dendrocnide moroides*) in Australia known as the "suicide plant" whose sting can last years and is so agonizing that it drives people to commit suicide after touching it.

592. There is an 800-square-mile (2,060 km²) area of land, Bi'r Tawīl, between Egypt and Sudan that neither country will claim, nor wants.

593. There is cyanide in apple seeds.

594. When he was a teenager, Mick Jagger bit off a piece of his tongue when he collided with another basketball player — changing the sound of his voice to what we know today.

595. When inhaling, we take in more air in one nostril than the other. It switches around periodically from one to the other.

596. When the BBC World Service began in 1932, they warned listeners to keep their expectations low, stating, "The programmes will neither be very interesting nor very good."

597. While 71% of Americans believe in Hell, only 0.5% think that they are likely to end up there, a survey found.

598. Women have twice as many pain receptors as men.

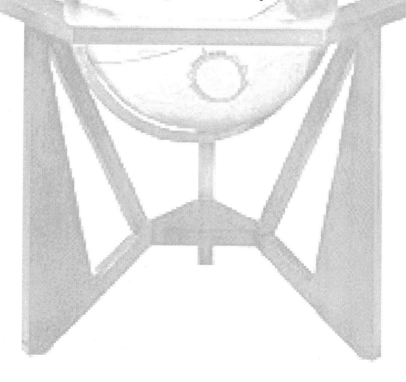

599. You breathe about 8,409,600 times in one year. (Unless you're dead, in which case you breathe considerably fewer times.)

600. You have a better chance of dying on your way to getting a lottery ticket than you do of actually winning the lottery.

Section Seven:
601–700

601-700

601. 100 million years ago, 6.5-meter-long primitive crocodiles were, as today, excellent swimmers. However, they were also capable, horrifyingly, of galloping at great speed across the plains.

602. 19th-century Hungarian composer and pianist Franz Liszt was the first musician reported to have women's underwear thrown at him.

603. 6 million pounds of syrup, worth $18 million USD, was stolen in 2013 from the Global Strategic Maple Syrup Reserve in Canada.

604. There is such a thing as the Global Strategic Maple Syrup Reserve in Canada.

605. A Belgian minister arrived by bike to a news conference to promote cycling in 2017, only to find, upon leaving half an hour later, that his bicycle had been stolen.

606. A Japanese man set up a CCTV camera in his kitchen to catch the thief stealing his food but discovered a homeless woman who had been living in his cupboard for over a year.

607. A man claiming to be a police officer over the telephone convinced the managers of over 70 restaurants and stores to strip-search their female employees. The scams happened over a period of 10 years until 2004, and such calls were reported in 30 U.S. states.

608. A single bat can eat up to 1,200 mosquito-sized insects an hour.

609. A sloth can take up to a month to digest food.

610. Adolf Hitler had only one testicle, and likely a deformed penis as well.

611. After being married for 7 years, a Brazilian couple found out they were actually brother and sister — whose mother left them in their infancy.

612. An elephant's skin can be up to 1 inch (2.54 cm) thick but is so sensitive it can feel a fly landing on it.

613. An estimated 46 million turkeys are eaten every Thanksgiving in the U.S.

614. Antarctica experiences 24 hours of sunlight in the summer and 24 hours of darkness during the winter.

615. Apple, Inc. has three times as much cash on hand as does the U.S. government

616. Approximately 90% of the fresh water on Earth's surface is held in the Antarctic ice sheet.

617. At roughly 250, Sudan has more than twice the number of pyramids you'll find in Egypt.

618. Bears have favorite trees and will walk for miles just to scratch their backs on them.

619. *Breatharianism* is the belief that food, and even water, are not necessary for survival, and that humans can be sustained solely by air. There are very few strict adherents

620. Camels have 3 eyelids.

621. Cats rub against people and furniture to mark their territory.

622. Charles Darwin ate a specimen of nearly every animal he discovered.

623. Clams can live for more than 400 years.

624. Deer can starve to death with a stomach full of hay.

625. *Districhiasis* is a rare condition where someone has two layers of eyelashes.

626. During a siege, the Mongols catapulted corpses that were infected with the plague over the city walls to infect the inhabitants.

627. Earth's core is as hot as the surface of the Sun.

628. Elvis Presley had a pet chimpanzee named Scatter.

629. Even after *That '70s Show* made her famous, Mila Kunis worked at a Rite Aid ice cream counter.

630. Fingernails grow almost 4 times faster than toenails.

631. For his role in *7 Years in Tibet*, actor Brad Pitt was banned from entering China.

632. France became the first country in the world to ban supermarkets from throwing away or destroying unsold food in 2016, forcing them instead to donate it.

633. Genius inventor and physicist Nikola Tesla swore by toe exercises. Every night, he'd repeatedly 'squish' his toes — 100 times for each foot.

634. Hawaii is the only place in the U.S. where coffee is commercially grown.

635. Humans and giraffes both have seven cervical (neck) vertebrae — those belonging to the giraffe are just longer.

636. During Mao's China in 1958, thousands of sparrows were killed because they were believed to be pests. As the sparrows decreased, locusts and other insects increased and ravaged crops in China. This led to the Great Chinese Famine, which killed 20–45 million people.

637. In 2000, a British pediatrician was forced to flee her home when some local residents mistook her job title to mean she was a pedophile, and vandalized her house.

638. In 2003, archaeologists in Venezuela discovered fossilized remains of a guinea pig the size of a cow.

639. In 2005, a psychologist and an economist taught a group of monkeys the concept of money. Soon, the monkeys engaged in prostitution.

640. In 2007, Scotland spent £125,000 devising a new national slogan. The winning entry was: "Welcome to Scotland".

641. In order for a new wolf cub to urinate, its mother has to massage its belly with her warm tongue.

642. In Quito, Ecuador, a group of hero vigilantes known as *"Acción Ortográfica Quito"* make it their mission to correct all the bad grammar they find in graffiti.

643. In Russia, Jews were believed to have had a secret vegetable they ate to prevent them from becoming alcoholics. Anti-Semitism was justified in this way, because the Jews refused to share their 'magic vegetable'. Whether the Jews ever did share their magic vegetable remains unknown.

644. In the 19th century, The U.S. Supreme Court unanimously decided that tomatoes were vegetables.

645. It is legal in France to marry a dead person. (And before you ask, no, you cannot 'consummate' the marriage.)

646. It would take 33 million people holding hands around the equator to make a full circle.

647. Jeff Goldblum was offered to be the voice of Siri by Steve Jobs himself but, sadly, declined.

648. KFC made a fried-chicken-scented SPF 30 sunscreen.

649. Max Planck's physics professor advised him against going into physics, saying, "In this field, almost everything is already discovered." Planck went on to become the initial founder of quantum theory.

650. Of human meat, according to convicted cannibal Armin Meiwes, "The flesh tastes like pork, a little bit more bitter, stronger. It tastes quite good."

651. Outer space is only an hour's drive away, if you somehow drive your car straight upwards.

652. *Photographs of Algae*, published in 1845, was the first book ever to contain photographs.

653. Princess Leia's iconic double-bun hairstyle, though disliked by actress Carrie Fisher, was inspired by Mexican rebel fighters, *soldaderas*, from the turn of the 20th century.

654. Rabbits are able to die of fright.

655. Radioactive substance Americium-241 is used in smoke detectors.

656. Research shows that in terms of bite attacks against people, dachshunds, or "wiener dogs", are more aggressive than pit bulls.

657. Scientists are developing "Gecko Gloves" that will allow you to climb up any wall.

658. Scientists have noticed that humpback whales around the world have been rescuing animals being hunted by orcas.

659. Scotland, then called Caledonia, was one of the few countries able to fend off being conquered by the Romans.

660. Skunks can spray as far as 10–15 feet, and up to 6 times in succession.

661. Snake Island, near São Paulo, is only 110 acres but hosts an estimated 4,000 snakes.

662. Sound travels 15 times faster through steel than air.

663. Steve McQueen's infidelity might have saved his life. He was supposed to attend the dinner party where the Manson family murdered Sharon Tate and others, but skipped it after he "ran into a chickie."

664. Sweden has their own national font, Sweden Sans, to "unambiguously represent Sweden in the world." This factoid is written in it.

665. The *Armillaria ostoyae* is one of the largest living organisms and colloquially known as the "Humongous Fungus" — with one specimen found to be covering 3.4 sq mi (8.8 km2).

666. The British Standards Institution has a 5,000-word report on the correct way to make a cup of tea.

667. The co-owner of Macy's died on the Titanic. He refused to get in a lifeboat before women and children, and his wife refused to leave without him. They were last seen standing on the deck, arm in arm.

668. The dolphin is the smartest animal after humans.

669. The durian fruit, known as the world's smelliest fruit, is so stinky that in parts of Asia

it is not allowed to be taken on buses or into hotels.

670. The EU forbade cheese made in Stilton to be called Stilton cheese.

671. The fact that we humans use only 10% of our brains . . . is a myth.

672. The FBI says that being a long-haul trucker is an ideal profession for a serial killer. Right now, there are no less than 25 long-haul truckers in prison for serial killings.

673. The FBI started amassing a file on Sacha Baron Cohen while he was filming *Borat* because of numerous complaints about a strange man traveling around the country in an ice cream truck.

674. The female lion does 90% of the hunting.

675. The Gombe Chimpanzee War was a 4-year violent conflict between two communities of chimpanzees in Gombe Stream National Park, in Tanzania.

676. The governmental system of democracy was introduced by the Athenians 2,500 years ago.

677. The longest recorded flight of a chicken is 13 seconds.

678. The mask worn by Michael Myers in *Halloween* is a William Shatner Captain Kirk mask painted white.

679. The middle finger of Galileo is on display in the Florence History of Science Museum. It stands erect — flipping the bird, so to speak.

680. The number of genetic material found in an organism doesn't determine how advanced it is.

681. The orange-colored carrot appeared in the 15th to 16th century. Previously, the roots of this plant were usually purple, yellow, black, and red

682. The 'paper' that paper money is printed on is made from cotton and linen — and so is not really paper at all.

683. The Sensorwake® is an olfactory alarm clock — using aromas of your choice to wake you instead of sound.

684. The tea bag was introduced in 1908.

685. The town of Whynot, North Carolina, has its name because as residents were arguing over a name for the town, someone stood up

and said, "Why not name the town Why Not and let's go home?" And so they did.

686. The U.S. has no official language.

687. The world's largest existing family consists of the husband, 39 wives, and 94 children.

688. There are more than 50 different kinds of Macropods (kangaroos, wallabies, and their kin) in Australia.

689. There are so many trees in London that it can be classified as a forest, according to a UN definition.

690. There's a synonym for the word "synonym": *poecilonym.*

691. Thomas Edison invented very few of the things people think he did. He had a small team

of people he would pay next to nothing to come up with ideas, which he would then patent and take credit for.

692. Tillie, a dog who painted, had over 17 solo exhibits under her collar, including shows in Milan, Amsterdam, and Brussels.

693. United Airlines once sued a 22-year-old man after he created a website to help people find cheaper flight tickets.

694. *Wasp* used to be "waps," while *bird* used to be "brid" and *horse* used to be "hros" — with pronunciation errors such as these making the English language what it is today.

695. When a border is disputed by two or more territories, Google Maps changes its borders in each country to reflect that country's beliefs.

696. When he was 16, Sir Isaac Newton threatened to burn his parents alive.

697. When United Airlines broke a man's $4,500 guitar and refused to pay for it in 2009, he wrote a protest song in response. Over the next 4 weeks, as the song became a hit on YouTube, United's stock price fell 10%, costing stockholders $180 million.

698. While filming Disney's *Napoleon and Samantha*, an 8-year-old Jodie Foster was mauled by a lion.

699. With the ashes of Dr. Eugene Shoemaker (geologist, astronomer) on the Moon, he becomes the first person to have been laid to rest on another celestial body.

700. You can get a splinter from hair and it is actually somewhat common (especially among barbers and hairstylists).

Section Eight:
701–800

701-800

701. "Jay" was a slang term for a foolish person. That is where the term "jay-walker" comes from.

702. "Nice" used to mean *accurate*.

703. 90% of the world's human population lives in the Northern Hemisphere.

704. A 2008 survey of British teenagers found that 58% thought Sherlock Holmes was a real person and 20% thought Winston Churchill was a fictional character.

705. A degree in bra studies can be attained at Hong Kong's Polytechnic University.

706. A doll named "Growing Up Skipper" was made by Mattel in the 1970s and when you rotated her left arm her breasts grew larger.

707. A flock of crows is known as a *murder.*

708. A large percentage of *Monty Python and The Holy Grail*'s budget was donated by the members of Led Zeppelin and Pink Floyd.

709. A single starfish arm can regenerate a whole new body.

710. About 1 million Japanese men are estimated to be locking themselves in their bedrooms for years, creating social and health problems — a condition called *Hikikomori.*

711.   About 10 million people visit the Great Wall of China each year.

712.   Air pollution in China can increase snowfall in California.

713.   Airplane food is relatively unappetizing because our sense of smell and taste decrease by 20–50% during flights.

714.   American soldiers were known as G.I. Joes during World War II. As they drank large amounts of coffee, the drink soon earned the name "a cup of Joe".

715.   An ad campaign for Kellogg's in 1907 offered a free sample box of cereal to any woman who would wink at her grocer.

716.   An estimated 40 million people in northern China live in a type of cave houses (yaodong 窑洞).

717. Ancient Egyptian ruler Pharaoh Pepi II purportedly hated flies so much that he would keep naked slaves smeared with honey near him in order to keep flies away from him (and attract them instead to his human flystrips).

718. Ancient Egyptians shaved off their eyebrows to signify their loss when grieving the death of their cats.

719. ATMs in the Vatican City have Latin as one of the language options.

720. Bananas are curved because they grow towards the sun.

721. Bees can sense the Earth's magnetic fields.

722. *Boanthropy* is a psychological disorder in which sufferers possess the udderly ridiculous conviction that they are cows.

723. Captain Morgan really existed. He was a Welsh pirate who later became Lieutenant Governor of Jamaica.

724. Casper the Friendly Ghost's family name is McFadden, making his proper name Casper McFadden.

725. Cleopatra was not Egyptian. She was Macedonian Greek.

726. Clinically speaking, people under the influence of power act as if they had suffered a traumatic brain injury.

727. Coffee beans are not beans — they are the fruit pits of a flowering evergreen tree.

728. Comedians and funny people, research has shown, are in general markedly more depressed than average.

729. *Derealization* is a peculiar dissociative phenomenon that causes the external world to feel dreamlike.

730. Dolphins have names for each other and can call for each other specifically.

731. Dr. Ruth Westheimer, the well-known sex therapist, was trained by the Israeli Defense Force to be a sniper.

732. Everything falls into one of two groups: It's either alive, or it isn't. Ever since scientists have known of viruses, they've been unable to successfully determine which of these two categories viruses belong to.

733. *Fibrodysplasia ossificans progressiva* is a progressive genetic disorder that turns soft tissues into bone over time, ossifying skeletal muscle and causing joints to fuse together.

734. Foam isn't classified as a liquid, a gas, or a solid, but it's all three at the same time.

735. *Green Eggs and Ham* uses only 50 different words. Seuss's editor bet him after *The Cat in the Hat*, which used 225 words, that Seuss couldn't write a book using fewer.

736. Heart attacks are more likely to happen on a Monday.

737. Hippos secrete a reddish substance from their skin that looks like blood but is actually a handy UV shield as well as a topical antiseptic.

738. Humans shed roughly 77 pounds of skin in their lifetime.

739. If you peel certain kinds of sticky tape (including Scotch tape) in a vacuum, it produces short bursts of X-rays.

740. In 1910 in the U.S., the Japanese water hyacinth had started clogging up waterways. There was also a meat shortage at the time. Two Louisiana men proposed an ideal solution: start a hippopotamus farm, as hippos loved to eat hyacinths and their meat was also tasty. Sadly, the idea was not embraced.

741. In 1939, Adolf Hitler's nephew, William, wrote an article entitled "Why I Hate My Uncle".

742. In 1988, an extreme case of the hiccups was cured by rectal massage.

743. In 1991, the voice actor for Disney's Mickey Mouse married the voice actor for Minnie Mouse.

744. In 1999, Google was willing to sell to Excite (better known today as Ask.com) for under 1 million but Excite turned them down.

745. In 2008, a stampede of Black Friday shoppers crushed a Walmart employee to death as they smashed through the front doors. The police officers who were trying to perform CPR were also trampled on by the crowd desperate for discounts.

746. In Australia, sex workers can deduct dance lessons, lingerie, cosmetics, and hair products from their taxes.

747. In China, an estimated 45 billion pairs of disposable chopsticks are produced yearly.

748. In Germany, breaking plates the night before the ceremony for good luck (*Polterabend*) is a traditional way of celebrating a couple's approaching wedding.

749. In the 1980s, A&W sold 1/3-lb burgers to rival McDonald's 1/4-lb burgers at the same price. But customers still preferred the

McDonald's burger because they thought 1/3 was a smaller fraction than 1/4, and so were convinced they were getting less meat with A&W's offering.

750. In the 1980s, Pablo Escobar's Medellín cartel was spending $2,500 USD a month on rubber bands to hold their stacks of bills together.

751. Indonesia's *kopi luwak*, or civet coffee, is the world's most expensive coffee, costing an average of $50 USD a cup — the coffee beans are collected from the feces of civet cats.

752. Japanese Team Ico's trio of games, *Ico, Shadow of the Colossus,* and *The Last Guardian*, are generally considered the most beautiful video games ever made, essentially elevating the medium to an artform.

753. Jethro Tull's Ian Anderson abandoned the guitar after hearing Eric Clapton play — concluding, in despair, that he'd never be as good at it as Clapton — and took up the flute instead.

754. Johannes Brahms, the great German composer and pianist, had such a dislike for cats that his favorite pastime was sitting on a large windowsill of his living room and shooting a bow and arrow at passing stray cats.

755. Johnny Cash's song "A Boy Named Sue" was penned by children's author Shel Silverstein.

756. Kids in the UK spend less time outside than prison inmates., according to a 2016 report.

757. *Koro* is a mass delusion in which people believe their genitals are shrinking or have been stolen entirely. It has overtaken entire towns and villages in several African countries.

758. Lucid dreaming is the experience of realizing, in your dream, that you are dreaming — along with the ability, to an extent, to control your dream.

759. Machine-spun cotton candy was invented in 1897 by the dentist William Morrison and was called, at the time, "Fairy Floss".

760. Nutella® hazelnut spread was invented by an Italian pastry-maker following WWII in response to the shortage of cocoa supplies.

761. On April Fools' Day of 1957, when the BBC had broadcast a hoax news report about

how spaghetti was grown from trees, hundreds of viewers called to find out more information about how they might grow a "spaghetti tree" for themselves.

762. On Good Friday, 1930, the BBC reported that, "There is no news."

763. Police in the northern Madhya Pradesh state of India get paid an allowance for growing a moustache.

764. Prairie dogs greet each other by 'kissing'.

765. *Pronoia*, the opposite of paranoia, is the delusion that everyone is secretly plotting your success.

766. *Pteronophobia* is the fear of being tickled by feathers.

767. Q-tips® were originally called Baby Gays.

768. Repetitive, obsessive nose-picking is called *rhinotillexomania*.

769. San Francisco has been referred to as "The City That Waits to Die" because of the imminent, inevitable threat of a massive earthquake.

770. Seahorses travel in pairs and hold each other's tails.

771. Sheep have been trained to recognize the faces of celebrities, including former U.S. President Barack Obama, and actors Emma Watson and Jake Gyllenhaal.

772. Shyness is thought to be an evolutionary adaptation: whereas the braver animals may find more mates and eat more food, the shyer

individuals, hiding on the sidelines, might avoid attack.

773. Sweden has more McDonald's per capita than any other country in Europe.

774. The "M&M" of M&M's chocolate candies stands for the initials of the company's founders, Mars & Murrie.

775. The average high school kid today has the same level of anxiety as the average psychiatric patient in the early 1950s.

776. The computer mouse was called "X-Y Position Indicator for a Display System" when it was first invented.

777. The country of Wales contains more castles per square mile than any other country in the world.

778. The distinctive sound created by Black Sabbath guitarist Tony Iommi was a result of him down-tuning his instrument to make it easier for him to play after several of his fingertips were cut off in an accident.

779. The Fatburger restaurant chain offers a sandwich called the "Hypocrite Burger" which is a veggie burger topped with streaks of delicious bacon.

780. The first organized municipal fire brigade in the world was established in Edinburgh, Scotland.

781. The Great Pyramid of Khufu at Giza is comprised of roughly 2.3 million stone blocks.

782. The Hoover Dam, in the U.S. state of Nevada, was built to last 10,000 years.

783. The hottest man-made temperature ever recorded is 7.2 trillion degrees F (about four billion degrees C).

784. The inventors of Bubble Wrap® first tried to sell their product as wallpaper.

785. The Isle of Mann has the oldest continuous parliament in the world.

786. The manuscript for *Curious George* was carried out of France by two men on bicycles just before the Nazi invasion.

787. The Nazi SS uniform was based on that worn by the Massachusetts State Police.

788. The population of Ireland is still 2 million less than it was before the Great Potato Famine of 1845–1852.

789. The raincoat was invented in 1824 in Scotland by Charles Macintosh. In Great Britain, the garment is still called a "Mac".

790. The world's longest piece of music — John Cage's composition for organ, "ORGAN2/ASLSP" (As SLow aS Possible) — lasts 639 years.

791. There is a "white man" café in Tokyo, where Japanese ladies ring a bell to summon tuxedo-wearing caucasians who respond with, "Yes, princess?" and serve them cake.

792. There was a Christmas truce (German: *Weihnachtsfrieden*; French: *Trêve de Noël*) along the Western Front of World War I in 1914, wherein French, German, and British soldiers crossed trenches to exchange seasonal greetings, talk, and swap food and souvenirs.

793. There was originally a fourth member of the Rice Krispies elves called *Pow!*

794. There's a 'sea organ' built on the coast of Croatia that plays music like an organ when waves crash in and out of it.

795. When Albert Einstein published his Theory of General Relativity, the *New York Times* sent their golfing correspondent to interview him.

796. When the Declaration of Independence was being drafted, Benjamin Franklin suggested that the word "sacred" be replaced with "self-evident" because he believed that the nation should be founded on reason and not faith.

797. When the mummy of Ramesses II was sent to France in the mid-1970s, it was issued

an Egyptian passport for travel. The Pharaoh's occupation was listed as "King (deceased)".

798. When you flip a coin, there is actually a 51% chance (as opposed to 50/50, as you might expect) it will land on the side that was facing up.

799. Wim Hof, of the Netherlands, is virtually impervious to cold. In January 1999, he traveled 100 miles north of the Arctic Circle to run a half marathon in his bare feet.

800. Woodingdean Well, in England, is 392 meters (1,285 ft.) deep — making it the deepest hand-dug well in the world.

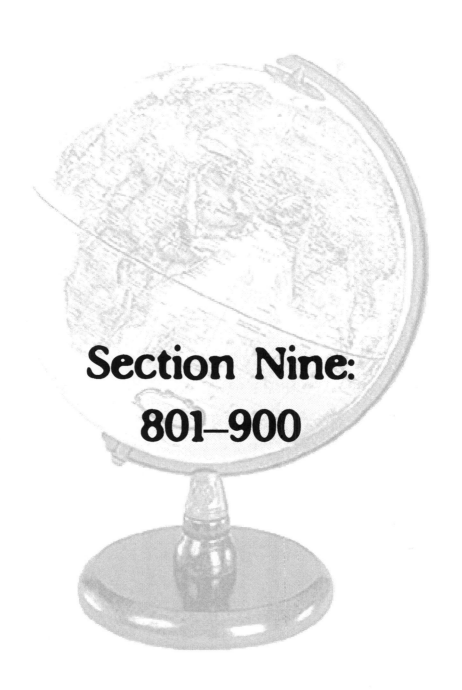

Section Nine:
801–900

801-900

801. "Million Dollar Point" is an area in the Pacific where the U.S. army dumped all its equipment after WW2 because it was cheaper than bringing it home.

802. "The Devil's Bridge" is a 19th-century structure in Kromlau, Germany, that was designed to make a perfect circle with its reflection in the water below.

803. "The quick brown fox jumps over the lazy dog" is an English-language pangram — a sentence that contains all of the letters of the alphabet.

804. 1 in every 2 million lobsters is born with a genetic defect that turns them a beautiful blue.

805. 87% of Americans can be uniquely identified using only three bits of information: ZIP code, birth date, and gender.

806. The bat is the only mammal that can fly.

807. A cow-smuggling tunnel was discovered in 2017 under the India–Pakistan border.

808. A group of bats is called a *cauldron*.

809. A group of buffalo is called an *obstinacy*.

810. A group of crabs is called a *consortium*.

811. A group of eagles is called a *convocation*.

812. A group of flamingos are called a *flamboyance*.

813. A group of larks is called an *exaltation*.

814. A group of lemurs is called a *conspiracy*.

815. A group of ravens is called an *unkindness*.

816. A group of starlings is called a *murmuration*.

817. A group of wild rabbits are called a *fluffle*.

818. A narwhal's tusk is actually an exaggerated front left tooth.

819. A wasp from the family Braconidae can be trained to detect many subtle scents, such

as the smell of explosives or drugs — and surprisingly, they are much easier to train than sniffer dogs.

820. According to the famous Greek physician Hippocrates, donkey milk can be used to cure numerous ailments including poisoning, liver troubles, fevers, and several infectious diseases.

821. Adult male bears will often kill and eat cubs, so, out of necessity, females find dens far away from the males.

822. After OutKast sang "Shake it like a Polaroid picture," Polaroid released a statement saying, "Shaking or waving can damage the image."

823. All clown fish, funnily enough, are born males but can turn female to reproduce.

824. Animals in the mammalian family of Tragulidae (chevrotains) look like cute, tiny little deer . . . with fangs.

825. As soon as tiger shark embryos develop teeth, they attack and eat each other in the womb.

826. Astronauts aboard Apollo 10 heard unexplained 'outer-spacey' music while orbiting the dark side of the Moon.

827. *Ayam Cemani* is an uncommon and relatively modern breed of chicken from Indonesia that is entirely black — inside and out.

828. Baby echidnas are called *puggles*.

829. Before becoming "Posh Spice", Victoria Beckham used to dress up as a sperm for a BBC sex-education show.

830. Blue jays can mimic the sound of a hawk to scare away other birds.

831. By the Middle Ages, black pepper had become a luxury item, so expensive that it was used to pay rent and taxes.

832. Chickens are the closest living relatives of Tyrannosaurus rex.

833. China produces and consumes almost 500 million swine a year, half of all the pigs in the world.

834. Dogs sneeze to show other dogs they are being playful.

835. During the 18th century, you could pay your admission ticket to the zoo in London by bringing a cat or a dog to feed the lions.

836. Elephant shrews are, oddly, related to actual elephants — and more closely related to elephants, in fact, than to other shrews.

837. Elephants are pregnant for nearly two years — the longest gestation period of any mammal.

838. Female Komodo dragons don't need a male to reproduce.

839. Fur seals like to have sex with penguins.

840. Giraffes have high blood pressure, which prevents fainting when raising their heads.

841. Gorillas can catch human colds and other illnesses.

842. Grizzly bears have a bite-force of over 8,000,000 pascals — enough to crush a

bowling ball if they should want to (you never know).

843. Honeybees can get sexually-transmitted diseases.

844. Horned lizards shoot blood from their eyes as a defense mechanism.

845. Horses are distantly related to rhinos.

846. Hugo Boss, founder of the luxury clothing line, was a Nazi who, from 1934, was an official supplier of uniforms to the SA, SS, Hitler Youth, NSKK and other Party organizations.

847. In 2009, Billy Joel's daughter tried to commit suicide by taking a large quantity of homeopathic pills. Miraculously, she survived.

848. In 2010, the fastest supercomputer in the entire U.S. Defense Department was built. It was primarily comprised of 1,760 PlayStation-3 processors.

849. In 2011, scientists found 2,368 species of bacteria that live in the belly button, 1,458 of which were new to science.

850. In April 2017, a Japanese man was arrested for having lived in the roof attic of a public restroom for 3 years.

851. In French, the term *puce* — literally meaning "flea" — is a term of endearment akin to "darling".

852. In the 1920s, several insect-related phrases existed to describe excellence. Of these, only "the bee's knees" survives today. For a time, however, "the flea's eyebrows" was also used to express admiration.

853. In the 1930s, a type of dog carrier was devised that could be fixed in place on a car's running board.

854. In the 1940s, England, because of wartime shortages, attempted to use whale as a substitute for more common types of meat. Taste-testers, however, were certain that even starving people wouldn't eat it.

855. It takes 3 to 4 years for a coffee tree to mature and, once it matures, it will bear 1 to 2 pounds of beans per growing season.

856. Judy Sheindlin, TV's Judge Judy, makes $45 million USD a year.

857. Just as human babies suck their thumbs, baby elephants suck their trunks for comfort.

858. Koala bears are not bears. They are marsupials.

859. Male capuchin monkeys pee on their hands and rub their urine all over their fur. Apparently, it makes them sexually appealing to the female capuchins.

860. Male kangaroos flex their biceps to impress females.

861. Male platypuses are venomous.

862. Male ring-tailed lemurs (an otherwise adorable, furry primate) have 'stink fights' wherein they rub the tips of their tails in their body's scent glands and then wave their tails, taunting each other.

863. Male turtles grunt and females hiss — much like humans.

864. Much like the fictional xenomorph creature from the *Alien* film series, moray eels

have a second set of jaws that extend from their throats.

865. Norway's Bouvet Island was discovered in 1739, then lost again for another 69 years.

866. Orcas, or killer whales, are actually a species of dolphin.

867. Ounce per ounce, nutritious food costs up to 10 times more than junk food.

868. Polar bears' fur insulates their body so effectively that virtually no outside heat can be detected by an infrared camera.

869. Researchers of Stockholm University found that chickens prefer beautiful faces.

870. Scientists have discovered crows are so intelligent that they actually play pranks on each other.

871. Sir Isaac Newton never had sex. He was fiercely Protestant, and would not have considered sex without marriage first. But he was too busy with mathematics.

872. Snakes have two penises (hemipenes) but, perhaps sadly for the snake, can only use one at a time.

873. Some cats can be allergic to humans.

874. Some lobster species can live up 50 years or more.

875. Technically, only male peacocks are properly called peacocks — females are called *peahens*, and together they are called *peafowl*.

876. The African penguin makes donkey-like sounds and is known as the "jackass penguin".

877. The annual Monkey Buffet Festival in Thailand provides food and drink to the local monkey population — more than 2,000 — thanking them for drawing tourists to the town.

878. The Atlantic bluefin tuna, when fighting fishermen, can have such high bursts of muscle activity that it can cook its own flesh.

879. The *axolotl* is a very cheerful-looking salamander species that can repair or entirely regenerate, if damaged, its limbs — and are thus used extensively in scientific research.

880. The brother of Adolf Dassler (founder of Adidas), Rudolf Dassler, was the more ardent Nazi of the two and went on to found another proficient sports company — Puma.

881. The Chinese soft-shelled turtle expels urine from its mouth. Meanwhile, the

Australian white-throated snapping turtle, also called the "bum-breathing turtle" can, as its name suggests, breathe through its anus.

882. The coldest permanently inhabited places in the world are the towns of Oymyakon and Verkhoyansk in Siberia. During winter, temperatures there average −50° F (−46° C).

883. The first webcam was built at Cambridge — to check the status of a coffee pot.

884. The founder of Adidas, Adolf Dassler (whose nickname was Adi), was a Nazi.

885. The French government gives medals to citizens who have "successfully raised several children with dignity."

886. The largest bat colony in the world is in Bracken Cave and is believed to consist of 20 million bats.

887. The nose print of a dog is like a fingerprint in that no two are alike.

888. The quokka, of Australia, is characterized as the happiest animal in the world.

889. The rainbow eucalyptus (*Eucalyptus deglupta*) is a tree native to the Philippines with a bark that is bright and multi-colored.

890. The Volkswagen (literally meaning "people's car") 'Beetle' was a Nazi-era vehicle presented by Hitler as a car that every German citizen could afford to buy.

891. There's a tree that's so poisonous, rainwater dripping off its leaves will burn your skin. It's called a *manchineel* tree.

892. Tigers have striped skin underneath their striped coats, and the stripes on a tiger

are like fingerprints in that no two patterns are the same.

893. Together, Americans, the French, and the Germans drink approximately 65% of the total coffee consumed in the world.

894. Trained pigeons can tell the difference between paintings by Picasso and Monet. (Whether they can recognize the difference between Monet and Manet remains unknown.)

895. Unlike the graying of human hair, the spots of a male giraffe will turn black as the animal ages.

896. Viruses can get viruses.

897. When squirrels forget where they've buried a stash of nuts, trees grow — with this nut dispersal of great benefit to the trees.

898. While mating, dragonflies form a heart shape with their tails.

899. Wombat feces are cube-shaped.

900. Women can fly airplanes in Saudi Arabia, but are not permitted to drive cars.

Section Ten:
901–1,000

901–1,000

901. 2.5 cans of Spam are consumed every second in the U.S.

902. A baby was born in 2005 with a conjoined head that had no body. The head could blink and smile.

903. A newspaper reporter, standing on an outdoor balcony of the White House, insulted the First Lady. President at the time Andrew Jackson shot the man in the chest and pitched his body over the rail.

904. A small amount of stress helps you to remember things better.

905. A solid-gold Thai Buddha statue was covered in plaster in the 18th century to hide its value from an invading army. The trick worked so well that everyone forgot it was really a gold statue — until an accident by movers revealed its secret again in 1955.

906. A study published in *Society & Animals* found that people are more empathetic toward dogs than fellow humans.

907. Actress Sigourney Weaver actually made the 'impossible basketball shot' in the *Alien: Resurrection* film.

908. An English horn is not English, and neither is it a horn — it is a French alto oboe.

909. An example of convergent evolution, two and three-toed sloths are not really related. Their appearance is so strikingly similar that even scientists were shocked to find out that the resemblance was purely coincidental.

910. Aside from humans, all of the great apes — gorillas, chimpanzees, bonobos, and orangutans — laugh when tickled.

911. Bees can be right or left-handed, just like humans.

912. Dung beetles roll balls of dung to impress prospective mates, just like humans.

913. Birds, even swallows, can't swallow particularly well. They rely on gravity to get their food & drink down, and is why you see them dip their beaks in water then lift their heads to let it trickle down.

914. Bonobos have been observed shaking their heads at each other to illustrate disapproval, just like humans.

915. Butterflies in your stomach is a stress response caused by adrenaline.

916. Camels, though herbivores, if they get very cross with you, are capable of crushing your skull with their massive jaws and sharp teeth.

917. Carrie Fisher never wore a bra with her Princess Leia costume.

918. Charles VIII (also known as Charles the Affable) had a 15-year reign as king of France between 1483 and 1498, before dying after hitting his head on a low doorway.

919. Charlie Sheen stayed awake for 48 hours prior to filming to look authentically wasted for

his cameo as a drugged-up felon in *Ferris Bueller's Day Off.*

920. Coelacanths were supposed to have become extinct in the Cretaceous period, along with the dinosaurs, but in 1938, a live specimen was caught by fishermen in South Africa.

921. Darth Vader only has 12 minutes of screen time in the original *Star Wars* film.

922. Despite global warming, we're still technically in an Ice Age.

923. Dubai scientists believe that the best way to cure genetic diseases is by modifying animals to produce curative proteins in their milk — with camels being the preferred animal.

924. *Fantasia* was supposed to be a short called *The Sorcerer's Apprentice*, but Walt Disney overspent on the production and decided to make it part of a full-length feature instead.

925. Gecko feet have millions of tiny hairs that stick to surfaces with a special chemical bond which helps them climb walls and hang on by just one toe.

926. Heath Ledger almost broke Jake Gyllenhaal's nose during the filming of a particularly rough kissing scene in *Brokeback Mountain*.

927. Human hair contains traces of gold.

928. Humans and kangaroos are, genetically, remarkably similar.

929. Humans were not smarter than Neanderthals, as it turns out. Homo sapiens, it seems, simply outlasted their *Homo neanderthalensis* cousins.

930. Hydrogen sulphide, the rather stinky component of flatus (farts), has been found to reduce high blood pressure when introduced into the circulatory system.

931. If you are an author in Norway, provided your finished book meets sufficient standards, the government will buy 1,000 copies and put them in libraries.

932. In 1930's Memphis, Tennessee, a method was devised to alert other motorists of particularly terrible drivers — special black license plates with a skull & crossbones on them.

933. In 1993 in Worcestershire, England, a Mr Karl Watkins, an electrician, was jailed for having sex with pavements.

934. In 2004, a woman had a heart attack on a plane full of doctors on their way to a cardiology conference.

935. In October 1975, 90% of Iceland's female population went on strike, demanding equal rights. They did not work, do housework, or look after their kids for an entire day.

936. In older versions of *Little Red Riding Hood*, the girl and the wolf eat Grandma together.

937. In Quentin Tarantino's film *Django Unchained*, Leonardo DiCaprio smashed his fist down onto a glass, causing him to bleed profusely. He calmly wrapped his hand while staying completely in character, continuing to

deliver his lines — with the scene being left as is and used in the film.

938. In the early 19th century, a trend of intentional train crashes began. It was meant to encourage people to take the train and boost ticket sales — and it did.

939. In the movie *Titanic,* the charcoal sketch of Kate Winslet's character you see being done in the film was actually drawn by director James Cameron.

940. It is possible for water to both boil and freeze at the same time.

941. It is possible to train yourself to improve your senses, even into the hyperacuity range.

942. Japanese research has concluded that moderate drinking can boost your IQ.

943. Jupiter's moon Europa and Saturn's moon Enceladus are believed to have liquid oceans under their icy crusts.

944. King Alexander ruled over Greece in the early 20th century, for only 3 years, before dying from a monkey bite.

945. *Le Chêne Chapelle* (The Oak Chapel) in Allouville-Bellefosse is an 800-year-old oak tree which had been carved out in the 1600s to house two chapels within its enormous trunk.

946. Macaques have learned how to fish. Although they hunt without tools, some of these monkeys in Indonesia have been spotted catching fish with their bare hands since 1998.

947. Men can lactate, just as women can, but only under extreme circumstances.

948. O.J. Simpson almost played the Terminator, but James Cameron thought his personality was too pleasant.

949. Octopuses have been filmed taking night-time strolls out of the water and onto the shore on the coast of Ceredigion in Wales, UK.

950. Once a sound wave reaches your ear, your brain can recognize it in just 0.05 seconds.

951. One of the sounds used for the velociraptors' vocalizations in the *Jurassic Park* film were tortoises mating.

952. Opal has been detected on Mars — which means there is (or has been) also water on Mars.

953. Originally, handshakes were to check that whoever you were meeting didn't carry a concealed weapon.

954. Pixar's *Up* (2009) was the first animated film to open at the Cannes Film Festival.

955. *Psycho* (1960) was the first American film to show a flushing toilet — quite shocking at the time for U.S. audiences.

956. Ravens 'protect' the Tower of London and have done since 1661, maintaining a continual presence there.

957. Ravens and crows can recognize and remember human faces, as well as remember if they like you or not.

958. Ravens have been seen sliding on snow with makeshift sleds made of bark.

959. Ravens like to get high. They smash ants and rub them all over their bodies. Ants produce formic acid when smashed, which is absorbed into the ravens' skin and apparently feels incredibly good to them.

960. Researchers at Yale New Haven Hospital found that monkeys like to gamble.

961. Scallops have approximately 100 eyes situated around the edge of their shell.

962. Scientists believe that dreaming about an activity can make you better at it.

963. Scientists have identified the chemical that suppresses unwanted thoughts in the brain.

964. Seahorses are covered in bony plates rather than scales.

965. Sean Connery wore a hairpiece in every one of his Bond performances.

966. Smokers are 3 times more likely to develop chronic back pain than non-smokers.

967. The actor Samuel L. Jackson first used the word "motherfucker" — now essentially his catch-phrase — to overcome a life-long stutter.

968. The Aussie state of Tasmania has the world's cleanest air.

969. The banana tree is not a tree — technically, it is an herb.

970. The burning-of-Atlanta scene in *Gone with the Wind* was done by burning old MGM film sets — that needed to be cleared from the back lot anyway.

971. The capybara of South America is the largest living rodent in the world. Fortunately, it is also one of the friendliest.

972. The Chinese giant salamander (Andrias davidianus) is the largest salamander and largest amphibian in the world, reaching a length of 180 cm (5.9 ft).

973. The *crakow* was a trendy shoe with an incredibly long toe, popular in 15th-century Europe. The length of the shoe's toe was an indicator of social status — the longer the toe, the higher the esteem.

974. The director of *The Notebook* wanted an actor that wasn't handsome to play Noah, so he cast Ryan Gosling.

975. The dragon's blood tree (*Dracaena cinnabari*), once pierced, produces a bright red

sap which oozes out. The sap is used as, among other things, a varnish for violins.

976. The Duesenberg Motor Company made very high-quality automobiles in the early half of the 20th century. As a result, it is believed the slang word "doozy" — referring to something extraordinary — was derived from the name Duesenberg.

977. The Earth's ozone hole is shrinking and is now the smallest it's been since 1988 — with the help of global efforts since the mid-1980s to ban the emission of ozone-depleting chemicals.

978. The film *Psycho* was released in B&W due to concerns the famous shower scene would be too much for audiences of that era to handle in more graphic color — but also to help get the scene past censors.

979. The goosander, a type of large duck, has a bill that contains more than 150 razor-sharp teeth, curved backwards, which can slice through the bodies of fish like a hot knife in butter.

980. The Harlan Ellison-scripted "The City on the Edge of Forever" is generally regarded as the finest of the original *Star Trek* episodes.

981. The Hercules beetle can grow big enough to easily cover a human hand.

982. The highest wave ever surfed was as high as a 10-story building.

983. The hippopotamus has the largest canines of any land animal, with two sword-like teeth that reach a monstrous 16 inches (40cm) in length.

984. The human nose (and brain) can detect and distinguish between roughly a trillion different smells.

985. The Komodo dragon can devour 5 pounds of meat in under 1 minute.

986. *The Lord of the Rings: The Return of the King* won all 11 Academy Awards it was nominated for.

987. The naked mole-rat (Heterocephalus glaber) are also known as "sand puppies".

988. The Norwegian Butter Crisis of 2011 resulted in prices for a pack of butter jumping to 300 Krone, or $50 USD.

989. The Overlook Hotel's carpet in *The Shining* and that found in Sid's house in the Pixar *Toy Story* film are nearly identical.

990. The payara, a fish that lives in the waters of the Amazon, has 3-to-4-inch fangs — which it uses to chomp through the vital organs of its prey.

991. The *Silent Hill* horror film is based in part off real-life Centralia, Pennsylvania — an old mining town that has been on fire for over 50 years.

992. The TV remote has been found to be the single dirtiest item in the typical home.

993. The word "girl" was originally a gender-neutral term for a child. Boys were called "knave girls," and girls were called "gay girls."

994. The word *astronaut* comes from the Greek words for "star" and "sailor" — ástron and nautes, respectively.

995. There is such a thing as a coffee enema.

996. To director Fritz Lang's dismay, Adolf Hitler and Joseph Goebbels were ardent admirers of his 1927 film, *Metropolis*.

997. Until 1913, children in America could legally be shipped by parcel post.

998. Viggo Mortensen took the role of Aragorn in the *Lord of the Rings* films in large part because his young son loved the Tolkien books so much.

999. Within just 3 days of its release, *The Hunger Games* became Lionsgate's highest-grossing picture.

1000. You can (if you are so inclined) buy eel-flavored ice cream in Japan.

Section Eleven:
1,001–1,100

1,001–1,100

1001. "Molding cockle bread" was an erotic 17th-century dance similar to twerking, in which young ladies would get up on a table, lifting their coats as high as possible, and shaking their buttocks back and forth as if "kneading dough with their arses." It was also customary for them to sing or recite some rhymes as they did so.

1002. A "redshirt" refers to an expendable character and is derived from the *Star Trek* original series, wherein crew members wearing red shirts were always, inexplicably, the ones to die on dangerous away-team missions — conveniently leaving the main characters of the show unscathed.

1003. A 2002 study showed that a New Caledonian crow could bend a piece of wire into the shape of a hook so that it could retrieve food from a narrow space. Young children were presented the same puzzle and were unable to match the mental dexterity of the crow.

1004. A captive beluga whale living with dolphins swapped her language for theirs and now makes vocalizations unique to dolphins.

1005. A company called Lifestyle Pets claims that they are able to breed hypoallergenic cats and dogs. Prices start at $6,950 USD.

1006. A misunderstood or misinterpreted word or phrase resulting from a mishearing of the lyrics of a song is called a *mondegreen*.

1007. A teenaged Judy Garland was, purportedly, repeatedly molested by cheeky Munchkins during the making of *The Wizard of Oz*, purportedly putting their hands up her dress and generally making her life miserable on set.

1008. According to a scientific study, this is the world's funniest joke:

> Two hunters are out in the woods when one of them collapses. He's not breathing and his eyes are glazed, so his friend calls 911. "My friend is dead, what should I do?" The operator replies, "Calm down, sir, I can help. First make sure that he's dead." There's a silence, then a loud bang. Back on the phone, the guys says, "Okay, now what?"

1009. According to astronauts, space smells like seared steak, burning metal, gunpowder, raspberries, and perhaps rum.

1010. African grey parrots are as smart as a 5-year-old human child.

1011. After petroleum, coffee is the world's second most valuable traded commodity.

1012. *Agalmatophilia* describes sexual arousal evoked by a statue, doll, or mannequin.

1013. Alien Hand Syndrome is a condition in which one's 'rogue' hand acts independently, grasping objects or moving in a way contrary to what the individual wishes — much like Bruce Campbell's character experiences in the *Evil Dead* films.

1014. An extremely rare case has occurred in the U.S. of a (California) woman becoming pregnant while already pregnant, with the mother giving birth to 'twins' who were not conceived at the same time.

1015. *Anatidaephobia* is the peculiar fear that somewhere, somehow, a duck is watching you.

1016. *Anthophobia* is the fear of flowers.

1017. Apps for Apes is an Orangutan outreach program that uses iPads to help keep orangutans engaged. The apes love them, generally sticking to children's games but also watching some nature documentaries.

1018. Astronomers have found a star, called iPTF14hls, that went supernova, managed to pull through, and then, 60 years later, went supernova all over again.

1019. Australia has a larger population of camels than Egypt.

1020. Australia's dingo fence is longer than the Great Wall of China.

1021. Beheading does not render instant death, and a severed head may retain consciousness for up to 10 seconds.

1022. Bowhead whales have evolved an auxiliary mouth-penis.

1023. Brian May, guitarist of Queen, is an astrophysicist.

1024. *Casu marzu* is a traditional Sardinian sheep milk cheese that contains live maggots. Intentionally.

1025. Catherine the Great appointed official foot-ticklers, who would pleasure her by tickling her feet while telling salacious stories or singing songs.

1026. Cleopatra was said to have bathed in donkey milk every day. She purportedly needed about 500 donkeys to produce the required amount of milk each day, to preserve her beauty and youthfulness.

1027. Edwin Tobergta of Hamilton, Ohio, was arrested in 2002 for having sex with an inflatable pumpkin that was part of a Halloween display.

1028. Escape artist Harry Houdini worked undercover for many years, spying on royalty and political leaders of Europe for the American and British governments.

1029. Explorers Lewis & Clark brought an African slave with them named York. When many of the tribes they met found York's blackness could not be scrubbed off, they revered the massively-built man as nearly a god — and the local women took turns 'entertaining' York in his tent, with their husbands' proud consent.

1030. Female cockroaches of the Thorax genus carry their nymphs under a winged canopy on the back. Using special fang-like mouthparts, the babies feed by slicing open their mother's back and drinking her blood.

1031. For centuries, one of the first things that many people entering Milan saw was a bas-relief of a woman shaving her pubic hair. This carving was placed on the eastern gate of the city named Porta Tosa. The bas-relief remained there until the 19th century.

1032. For over 50 years, magician James Randi offered $1 million U.S. dollars to anyone who could demonstrate genuine supernatural or paranormal ability. No one was successfully able to claim it.

1033. Foreign Accent Syndrome describes a condition that causes a person to suddenly begin speaking spontaneously in a foreign accent, even if they'd never been previously exposed to that accent.

1034. *Formica rufa*, also known as the red wood ant, southern wood ant, or horse ant, are able to spray formic acid from their abdomens as a defense.

1035. Georgia O'Keeffe's paintings of flowers are generally regarded as stylized depictions of the female genitalia.

1036. Global warming 'solved' a land dispute between India and Bangladesh when the island in question disappeared underneath the waves.

1037. Head transplants are possible, and in fact have already been performed on monkeys.

1038. If you fold a paper in half 103 times, it'll be as thick as the observable Universe.

1039. In 2010, a Massachusetts genomics company mapped Ozzy Osborne's DNA in an effort to discover what sort of 'magical' helix construction may have enabled him to ingest massive, absolutely astonishing amounts of drugs & alcohol throughout his lifetime and yet, remarkably, still be alive.

1040. In an isolated village in the Dominican Republic, about 1 in 50 children are born appearing to be girls but grow male genitalia during puberty. They are known as *Guevedoces*, which effectively translates as "penis at twelve."

1041. In captivity, ravens can learn to talk better than a lot of parrots can. Ravens can also replicate wolves, other birds, garbage trucks, and even toilets flushing.

1042. In China, 'virgin boy eggs' are a delicacy. Each year in the spring, eggs are boiled in the urine of young virgin boys, usually aged ten and under.

1043. In England, if you're "having a butcher's" at something, it means you're having a look.

1044. In Nice, France, there is a café in which customers who order their coffee politely are charged less than those who don't. Those who order coffee with a *bonjour* and a *s'il vous plaît* are charged €1.40 ($1.93 USD). Coffee ordered with no greeting but with *s'il vous plaît* costs €4.25 ($5.85), and coffee ordered simply as *un café* costs €7 ($9.63).

1045. In November 2017, Seattle Seahawks fans were so loud they caused a spike in seismic activity equivalent to that of a microearthquake.

1046. In recent years, criminals from indigenous minority groups in Siberia have been outrunning Russian police by employing 'getaway reindeer'.

1047. In the U.S. state of Oregon there was a natural stone formation called "Cock Rock" because of its extraordinarily phallic appearance — until, sadly, it was renamed due to delicate sensibilities.

1048. Ines Ramirez Perez, a peasant living in Rio Talea, Mexico, is believed to be the only woman in the world who has performed a successful caesarian section on herself (in March 2000) and survived.

1049. Instead of kissing, mothers of the Manchu tribe used to show affection by sucking their child's penis in public, as kissing was considered a much too sexual display.

1050. It has been estimated that at least 40 nuclear warheads have been lost since the Cold War. Whoops-a-daisy.

1051. *Kimchi* is a fermented cabbage dish very popular in South Korea. When nappa cabbage rose in price by nearly 500% in 2010, newspapers dubbed it "a national tragedy" and "a once-in-a-century crisis."

1052. Koalas have fingerprints — fingerprints that are so human-like, in fact, that crime scene investigators can easily get them confused.

1053. Koko the gorilla (currently aged 46) began to learn sign language when she was a year old, and has since learned to communicate about 1,000 signs, as well as understand roughly 2,000 English words.

1054. Laika, a stray dog from the streets of Moscow, was the first living creature to orbit Earth — in the Soviet spacecraft *Sputnik 2*.

1055. Marmite, the distinctive English toast spread, is made as a by-product of the beer-making process.

1056. *Mesodinium chamaeleon*, a single-celled organism found off the coast of Scandinavia is, in turns, both an animal and a plant.

1057. No one knew how Casper the Friendly Ghost, as a human child, had expired until it was revealed in 1995 that he'd been a young adolescent who'd gone sledding all day and died of pneumonia.

1058. Only 0.07% of the U.S. federal prison population are atheists. The overwhelming majority of the remaining 99.3% are Christian.

1059. *Pareidolia* is the tendency to perceive a specific, often meaningful, image in a random or ambiguous visual pattern — such as Jesus, for instance, on a grilled-cheese sandwich.

1060. Play-Doh started out, in the 1930s, as a wallpaper cleaner.

1061. Ravens have been observed pretending to hide food in one place before quietly hiding it in another to throw off other ravens.

1062. Researchers at Lund University in Sweden conducted an experiment that involved trading with ravens and then cheating them to see if they'd remember. They did indeed remember.

1063. Roald Dahl, the well-known British children's author, wrote the screenplay for the Bond film *You Only Live Twice.*

1064. *Rogue Ales Beard Beer* is an American wild ale brewed by Rogue Ales of Newport, Oregon using wild yeast originally cultured from beard hairs belonging to Rogue Ales' brewmaster John Maier.

1065. Romantic love, it turns out, is biochemically indistinguishable from having a severe obsessive-compulsive disorder.

1066. Scientists have sequenced the entire genome of the tardigrade (AKA water bear) and the results suggest this creature has the most foreign genes of any animal studied so far — roughly 1/6th of the tardigrade's genome was stolen from other species.

1067. Scientists in Israel have created a prototype for a breed of featherless chicken that can save time on plucking, are more environmentally-friendly, and may in general significantly reduce the cost of raising them.

1068. Scientists want to introduce global warming on Mars to make life habitable for colonization.

1069. Sergeant Stubby, a pit bull breed, was the first war dog used by the United States in World War I. He is noted as being the only dog to be promoted to sergeant through combat.

1070. Stalin's first son shot himself because of his father's harshness toward him, but survived. Stalin said, "He can't even shoot straight."

1071. Stewart Copeland, drummer for The Police, composed the soundtracks for the first 3 *Spyro the Dragon* games from Insomniac Games.

1072. Students as young as 6 must use a 2,500-ft, rickety, bamboo ladder to attend a school in China's southwest Sichuan Province.

1073. Suresh Sakharkar of India spent 2 years training his pet parrot, Hariyal, to insult and swear at his stepmother. Hariyal offended the woman every time she walked past Sakharkar's home.

1074. Tardigrades are tiny creatures that are virtually indestructible — able to withstand extreme heat, extreme cold, immense pressure, and the vacuum of space among other things.

1075. Tashirojima (田代島) is a tiny island in Japan that is inhabited, though the human population is quite small. It has become known as "Cat Island" due to the exceedingly large stray cat population that thrives there (as a result of the local belief that feeding cats will bring wealth and good fortune).

1076. Taylor Wilson, an Ann Arbor, Michigan boy of 14, built a working nuclear fusion reactor in his grandmother's garage.

1077. Tears caused by sadness, happiness, and onions look different under the microscope.

1078. Thanks to Mustafa Kemal Atatürk, in 1935 there were 18 women MPs in the Turkish parliament when women in most other countries didn't even have the right to vote.

1079. The *black sapote* is a fruit native to Mexico that, when ripe, the inside bears a consistency and taste similar to that of chocolate pudding.

1080. The Cookie Monster doesn't actually eat cookies — he eats rice crackers, as they are much easier to clean and less likely to cause damage to the valuable puppet.

1081. The distinctive sound of the *Doctor Who* Tardis materializing was originally created by dragging ordinary house keys across the bass strings of an old piano, and playing the resulting sound backwards.

1082. The *jabuticaba* is a fruit tree native to Brazil, unusual in that its fruit grow all over the trunk — directly from its trunk — and not just in the branches, making it look like the tree is extruding oily tears.

1083. The Muppets had a regular spot on the first season of *Saturday Night Live*.

1084. The renowned film critic Roger Ebert famously stated, in 2006, that video games were not and could never be an artform. After a tsunami of criticism from video game enthusiasts, he finally relented (somewhat).

1085. The shortest scheduled flight in the world is 1.5 miles (2.4 km) long, from Westray to Papa Westray in the Orkney Islands of Scotland. The journey takes 1 minute 14 seconds to complete.

1086. *The Simpsons* cartoon has a hidden *McBain* movie hidden throughout several series. Individually, the clips are very short and seem like nothing more than time-fillers within episodes. But pulled out and placed together, they form a coherent film.

1087. The surrender of U-boat U-570 remains the only time a submarine has surrendered to an aircraft.

1088. The technological singularity is the point at which AI becomes smart enough to think as well as (or better than) humans, and begins to improve itself and self-replicate.

1089. The 'Wilhelm scream' is a stock sound effect of a man screaming that has been used in more than 360 movies and countless television series, beginning in 1951 for the film *Distant Drums*.

1090. There are tiny mites living on your eyelashes feeding on your skin cells and sebum, laying eggs, and defecating.

1091. There is a festival celebrated in Nepal for dogs called *Kukur Tihar*, honoring their loyalty and friendship.

1092. There is a rare medical condition known as *hereditary sensory autonomic neuropathy* — the lack of ability to feel pain.

1093. There is a species of worm known as the "pigbutt worm" or as the "flying buttocks" (Chaetopterus pugaporcinus) and it very much resembles a disembodied pig's bum.

1094. Though a group of ravens is called an "unkindness," ravens are highly empathic. A study published in 2010 found that ravens console the victim of an act of aggression.

1095. Toward the end of the 19th century, cocaine-laced tampons were sold to women, with claims as a cure-all. They were, as you can imagine, wildly popular while they lasted.

1096. *Turophobia* is the (quite unfounded) fear of cheese.

1097. U.S. President George Washington, suffering from an infection, was bled out by his three attending physicians, had blisters administered and vomit induced, and was also given an enema, among other ministrations. The doctors were mystified when Washington failed to recover and subsequently died.

1098. Violet Jessop, an Irish emigrant, was an ocean-liner stewardess that survived three separate disasters on Olympic-class ocean liners — *RMS Olympic, RMS Titanic,* and *HMHS Britannic.* She's either very lucky or very unlucky, depending upon your POV.

1099. When Koko the gorilla's pet cat was hit and killed by a car, Koko used her sign-language abilities to convey how upset she was.

1100. While in office, U.S. President Ronald Reagan sliced a large gash in his thigh with a chainsaw while working at his ranch.